THE SECOND COMING of REB YHSHWH

The Rabbi Called Jesus Christ

Carlo Suarès

Translation by Ferris Hartman

SAMUEL WEISER, INC.
York Beach, ME

First published in 1994 by
Samuel Weiser, Inc.
P. O. Box 612
York Beach, ME 03910–0612

Library of Congress Cataloging-in-Publication Data

Suarès, Carlo.
    [Mémoire sur le retour du rabbi qu'on appelle Jésus. English]
    The second coming of Reb Yhshwh : the rabbi called Jesus Christ /
by Carlo Suarès.
        p.   cm.
    Includes bibliographical references (p. xxx-xxx) and index.
    1. Jesus Christ—Miscellanea.   I. Title.
BT304.93.S913   1994
232–dc20   94–18308
                                                                    CIP

ISBN 0–87728–818–6
MV

Cover design by Fahrenheit

Printed in the United States of America

99 98 97 96 95 94
10 9 8 7 6 5 4 3 2 1

Typeset in 11 point Palatino

The paper used in this publication meets the minimum requirements of
the American National Standard for Permanence of Paper for Printed
Library Materials Z39.48–1984.

THE SECOND COMING of REB YHSHWH

I will tell a tale of time and duration, of space and measures, of sound and light, of achievements and frustrations. I will tell it for your benefit for fear you would not understand that which is of no time and no space, of no past or future and, in very truth, of no word—so that no tale would be told.

Do not forget that all tales are only tales. Would that mine be tantamount to the conveyance of a glimpse of that which is!

Table of Contents

Preface

The supernatural Jesus Christ—who made 2,000 years of history—is now undergoing a certain change. While "Christ" is becoming more and more impersonal and metaphysical, "Jesus"—under the double pressure of historical criticism and the priority that more and more people give to the social revolution—is becoming a solid figure like any other, totally devoid of mystery.

For some people, Jesus was merely a ringleader who took an active part in the tragic and desperate revolt of the Jews against Rome. Resting on a purely symbolic genealogy (3 x 4 generations after Abraham in the line of King David, and 20 generations from Abraham back to the mythical Adam), their Jesus of royal descent believed himself to be the Messiah come to bring a "for-all-time" victory to the Jews. In their view, he failed to do so and fell back to preaching a commonplace morality and healing the sick. His armed band, they claim, degenerated into a gang of thieves and killers, and he fled, trying in vain to avoid being caught and convicted.

For others, Jesus was a socialist, a Marxist, or an anarchist ahead of his time. He was prosecuted and condemned for his revolutionary activities. For some people, Jesus—materializing from nobody knows which Eastern stock or country, and with nothing in common with Israel—came to bring to the West some ancient, traditional philosophy of India or elsewhere. For others, Jesus was just one of Israel's lesser prophets. He merely repeated what Jewish tradition had known all along.

The Church, of course, reacts against such "theses," and theses are what they really are, despite supporting historical and philosophical proof. In this Babel of the deaf the Church can only say no, let itself be swept into the social stream and refuse the political, lean on the metaphysical, and allow the mythological to crumble away. Rooted in the archaic, and weighed down by centuries of alluvion, its doctrine is powerless to silence these criticisms with any telling arguments. This is due to the fact that the interpreters, whether historians or philosophers, may be able to expound their own points of view but fail to demonstrate how the others are wrong. When they reject the historicity of Jesus as revealed in the Gospels, the Acts, and the Epistles, each exponent has his or her own reasons for doing so, and reads the texts for the sole purpose of proving his or her own story to be the true one.

We are finally faced with various romanticized tales in which the character of Jesus is described in completely different ways, but in which he is always viewed in a "rational" light. One might wonder if rational thought can ever free Jesus from the supernatural on which the Church's doctrine rests. My answer to this question is an unequivocal "no," because the rational and irrational are not on the same level and do not meet. Times have changed. The irrational of 2,000 years ago might well become the rational of today. It need not fall into the absurd. On the other hand, the rational of the last century can become irrational and false tomorrow.

It was not necessary to make the Rabbi called Jesus a murdered God. It belittled Israel's incarnation and led to the adoration of a dead body, a cadaver. For centuries, the fathers of the Church have done their best to separate Israel from its essence. If the Church "falls into this dead body"[1] in this memoir, I hope to give it reasons to live. And I hope to give some to the Jews, too.

We are on the threshold of stupendous psychic changes that require an agonizing reappraisal of the data of

---

[1]"Jesus said: Whoever has known the world has found a corpse, and whoever has found a corpse, of him the world is not worthy." L. 56, *The Gospel According to Thomas* (New York: Harper & Row, 1959).

human consciousness centered on our spatiotemporal continuum. Such data close out the worlds beyond our dimensions and call themselves "rational." Or else they offer dreams of worlds beyond and project them into supernatural "heaven and hell" areas. The Rabbi came to "fulfill the scriptures," not to reject them. He came to explode the energy contained in Israel since the days of Abraham, and he came for no other purpose. It is useless to talk about it if one does not go back to the origins.

Today we can readily believe that the visitations of Moses and Elias on the summit of Mount Tabor where the Rabbi went to meet them were real; that Moses and Elias did actually turn up, personally, in bodies made of substances different from those of our palpable universe, but rendered visible. They not only entrusted Jesus with his mission but also gave him the means of carrying it out and passed on to him the prodigious Cosmic Energy they knew how to handle. Consequently the words of Jesus, his teaching, his parables, his acts became secondary, because his true mission was to produce this energy (which I hope to make you somehow perceive).

But the time was not ripe. The Rabbi knew it and he said so. There is a direct relationship between knowledge and the state of maturation of psychisms, the interpenetration of multidimensional worlds, consciousness and fundamental energies, the way time and space appear in an indefinite number of conscious levels while obeying a similar law, the direct action of thought on what used to be called matter; in short, everything that defines the quantum of action relating to a psychic change—all of which was unknown in the Rabbi's time, is still not known by the masses, and is the subject of the most advanced scientific research. On all sides metapsychic, psychokinetic phenomena, transmissions of thought, remote hypnotism, extrasensory perceptions, precise recollections of former lives, premonitions, et cetera, shatter the notion that such things are supernatural and demolish our mythologies.

The crack in our daily world—in the so-called rational thought that takes concrete and material form within a projection limited to three-dimensional space and to one-way linear time—was created by the Rabbi and has become a huge gap through which the Spirit of Truth is already breaking.

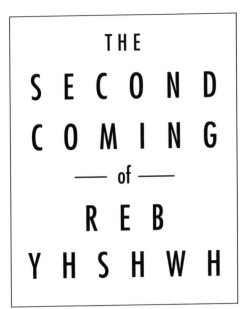

THE

SECOND

COMING

— of —

REB

YHSHWH

Chapter 1

MULTIDIMENSIONAL WORLDS

I WISH TO WRITE ABOUT AN EVENT THAT HAS been going on for some time now; about a stupendous, illimitable flux; about a mutation of psychisms; about the decisive turning point in human history. Such a project should first present everything humanity has known and believed (including everything it now knows and believes) and then transform the sum of it all into a single act of spontaneous, timeless consciousness. This would seem impossible if it were not for the fact that some people already perceive the event directly.

It is becoming more and more evident that the universe we see, measure, analyze, and believe in as a spatio-temporal continuum (three dimensions of space plus one dimension of linear time) is very far from being all that is. Space and time, which our minds call "objective," are actually only the inventions of an earthbound consciousness that, from mineral to human functions on one, two, or three dimensions—the third encompassing the first two and never going beyond.

Humanity today is finally discovering that an indefinite number of universes function in an indefinite number of dimensions. These universes coexist and penetrate each other. They both encompass and go beyond "our" universe. Without exception the fundamental error of our religions—and the "original sin" of human thinking—is that they can conceive universes in which there exist beings with multidimensional perceptions only in imaged, sensorial, or materialized forms.

What the Rabbi called Jesus came to show us is that there reside in these universes beings whose consciousness goes beyond the notion that they are individuals limited to their physical bodies. (Humans, according to some of our scientists, are constituted merely of what is between the tips of our toes and the top of our heads.) The Rabbi came to show us that among such beings, individuated, live our true selves: our souls.

The world in which we appear as "flesh and bones" is a world that is limited, projected, and created by a consciousness that is limited, projected, and created by that same world. These bodies—ours and those of all "solids," stars, and objects—are made of a void or vacuum, and exist only within our own coordinates. Beings coming from more complex coordinates pass through what we call "matter" without perceiving it, just as countless electromagnetic, cosmic, and other currents pass through us.

Our real selves, far from being this false evidence that brings such pressure to bear on us with problems and conflicts in our daily lives, are to be found in the nondimensional "indetermination" of the totality of that which is. This totality adds up to the indeterminate number of universes mentioned above. No dividing walls separate the graded mentalities of these universes. That is undoubtedly the most important thing the Rabbi has told us, even though he said it in symbolic terms—the only terms that then had a chance of being understood. But their meaning has been—and still is—twisted in a way that is fatal to human understanding.

No dividing walls exist between a superior consciousness and a vegetable consciousness: the bread and the wine are "the flesh and blood" of him who speaks. This does not mean that the sacred host taken with wine is the "flesh and blood" of that man. Far from it! Such a mixture of cannibalism and theophagy is abomination to the Rabbi. To eat a cracker, call it holy, and imagine that this is the "True Presence" is both primitive and barbarous.

No dividing walls exist between our daily consciousness and the most exalted consciousness: "Be ye therefore perfect, even as your Father which is in heaven is perfect"

(Matthew 5:48).[1] Stripped of symbolic images, this sentence and thousands of others state badly what the man who is called Jesus or some other name was trying to say. Paul put it this way to the Corinthians: "Know ye not that ye are the temple of God, and that the Spirit of God dwelleth in you?" (I Corinthians 3:16).

If I, in turn, try to say it more clearly, am I at fault, or am I "wise in [my] own conceits" (Romans 12:16)? Certainly not. I say what I have to say, regardless of what anyone might think of me, knowing that I am "one of his own" (in his consciousness), that he is in me and I in him, in him alive, in him who never rose vertically from Jerusalem to a fancy sky where he is supposed to be domiciled, in him on earth, neither dead nor risen from the dead, but simply alive.

And it is not in his name that I speak, nor in my name either. My words mean what dictionaries say they mean. I select and weigh them carefully. For me they have the value of a last will and testament. I could not leave this world without having formulated them precisely. Many of these words have already been published in my writings and spoken in my lectures. I owe it to myself to repeat them here, perhaps with more precision, and in a way that will seem aggressive, offensive, and violent to some. A nail has never been hammered solidly in with euphemisms. And the mundane ecumenical discourses that prevail in our many assemblies (wordy speakers and bored listeners) are only deceitful havens, voicing the 100 ways of serving up the Revelation so that it disturbs no one.

---

[1]References to the Bible are from the *King James* version.

Chapter 2

FAITH AND CREED

THE RABBI, *ALIVE*, IS DISTURBING. HOW BETTER TO neutralize him than by worshiping the effigy of a corpse nailed to a cross? What an extraordinary projection of unavowed guilt!

Is it a sin not to obey the Gospel? Certainly not. Isn't a man responsible to his own family? But the Rabbi called Jesus renounced his mother and brothers (Matthew 6:34). Can one love without discrimination? "But I say unto you, 'Love your enemies' " (Matthew 5:44).

Isn't blind faith enough? Must there be understanding, too? For Paul, his faith was simply his affirmation of the evidence at hand. He not only had seen the Rabbi in a semiphysical appearance on the road to Damascus, but also had received a vital shock from the penetration of the Rabbi's multidimensional universe into his daily world. However, this irruption did not free him from his Mosaic conditioning. His thinking remained bogged down in the archaisms of the laws of Moses—archaisms he bequeathed to the Church.

From disaster to disaster, from archaic mythology to symbols, to images to idolatry to iconolatry, the Church has transformed faith into creed instead of letting its temporality die in the "Intemporal." In terms of our space-time continuum, it has materialized that which is beyond time and space. And therein lies its unacknowledged guilt.

Faith is direct perception of the immortality of consciousness. It is the living mind's realization that it has projected itself into a mortal state although knowing itself to be immortal. This mortal state is unconscious, imaginary. It roams the face of the earth, enclosed within the miniconsciousness called "the human condition."

Reality is recognized only after resurrection. This resurrection precedes what is called "death." The Rabbi's resurrection came before his feigned death, a death which we
must die, but one that is impossible for us to die—because,
when we think of it, it is always behind us!

Creeds and beliefs are the opposite of faith. At first,
belief seems like a good bargain. "Believe, and you will be
rewarded; don't believe, and you will be punished."
Believing is on this side of death. Faith is on the other side.
"Therefore, if any man be in Christ, he is a new creature:
old things are passed away; behold, all things are become
new" (II Corinthians 5:17). This quotation and the words,
"If any man be in Christ," lead me to declare myself
emphatically as being *in* Reb YHSHWH, the Rabbi called
Jesus. Consequently, I obstinately obey his injunction to his
disciples to "tell no man that he was Jesus the Christ"
(Matthew 16:20). This clear statement means to me that he
strongly objected to being taken for a Christ.

He had chosen to come in a Hebrew body, and he was
a rabbi. I am a Hebrew myself through both parental lines,
and the word *Christ* is as alien to me as it was to him in that
incarnation: Israel incarnate, Israel made flesh. The word
Christ comes from the Greek. Through many centuries of
mythology is has acquired a fantastic meaning. Obviously
it did not fit Reb YHSHWH, the Rabbi Jesus. Let those who
accept every word of the Scriptures as accurate in every
language and translation take responsibility for such belief.

Chapter 3

THE PAST WITHOUT LIFE

SPIRIT HAS BEEN TAKING A BEATING FROM ECCLE-siastical cogitations for the last 2,000 years. For example: the adoration of the bleeding corpse of a man who died in anguish; the name Jesus Christ and its worship (but Jesus said, "Why callest thou me good? there is none good but one, that is, God" [Matthew 19:17]); and the promotion of fear with its guilt complexes, threats of eternal punishment, and desperate pleadings for mercy.

Such blows only petrify (oh! Peter) the psyches in a pseudospirituality that searches vainly for safety in a pseudosalvation bearing the Greek label *Christ*. I know that these words are clear only to those who are able to receive them directly. For those who understand me and for those who do not, let me add that if you use the word *God*, you should first have the intelligence and integrity to find out what you are talking about.

I am willing to accept the definition that God is consciousness, life, the source of all that is. And just as there are no divisions of temperature (the dividing measurements called degrees of temperature are only variations of the one temperature and exist as many separate figures only to those who invent or accept the figures), so Consciousness is One. Thus, being *in* him simplifies matters. Gone is the corpse to be worshiped. Gone is the consecrated wafer to be swallowed. And gone is the "creature" to swallow it. Gone, too, is a Christ who had been relegated to some faraway place called heaven. We in him, and he in us: one. Thus the quotation from II Corinthians 5:17 can be modified to read: "If any person is in Reb YHSHWH [to give the Rabbi Jesus his correct name], old things are passed away; behold, all things are become new."

Yes, everything becomes simple, almost too simple. The "new" comes when the "old" dies. We become "new creatures" by dying to ourselves. Misunderstood, that formula has led billions of times to death as *petrifaction—the* opposite of what the injunction means.

Only the "poor in spirit" understand without explanations, and "theirs is the kingdom of heaven" (Matthew 5:3).

Chapter 4

MISUNDERSTANDINGS AND BAD TRANSLATIONS

RECENTLY SOME FRIENDS INVITED ME TO THEIR home to meet a Franciscan. They imagined that we would have many interesting things to discuss together. "How happy I am to meet you, especially since I, too, am one of the companions of St. Francis," I said when we were introduced. Then I added, "We rejoice now, don't we, that we are in the Second Coming of Christ." (I was careful to use his Christian terminology.)

The man stared at me without a word. I could see that he was thinking, "There are many such madmen in lunatic asylums." Finally he replied, sternly but cautiously (I might be the dangerous type), "Don't you know that the Christ will not return until the end of the world? Haven't you read the Scriptures?"

Now it was my turn to stare in silence. I found myself thinking, "The end of the world? The end of the world? The end of the world? Which one of us is crazy?" Then I braved a question. "What is your occupation?" I asked.

"I am a scholar in Franciscan studies," he answered.

He had already turned his back on me and was engrossed in an elaborate dialogue about yoga exercises with an Asiatic guest. I thought to myself, "This 'end of the world,' what a spurious shelter! What have they done to sweet St. Francis? Scholars, are they? What is there to study in his love?"

That little scene made me aware of a prevalent tendency among people today: the importance they give to a statement depends upon the importance they give to the person who states it. In matters of the Church, the priority of importance is given first to antiquity, especially when it is supported by long-established tradition. It becomes hypnotic when the Church imposes it on weak minds with fearsome threats. I suggest, therefore, that we should not rely totally on any ancient texts, especially those labeled "holy," "sacred," or "the Word of God." Caution is all the more to be recommended if the text is presented in translation and not in its original language. Translations are frequently *mis*-translations. Even the original work must be read with discretion. Words can change their meanings from one century to the next. And the older the text, the more adulterated it may become through inaccurate copies made by ignorant, careless, or dishonest scribes.

Thoughts must be evaluated according to the times and circumstances in which they were written. Plato's *Republic*, which seemed so revolutionary in its time and situation, today sounds conservative even to hardened reactionaries.

One need only read the Gospels to discover that Jesus was conditioned by his time and by his role as Rabbi. There are many examples of this. For one, Matthew 5:22, "But I say unto you, That whosoever is angry with his brother without a cause shall be in danger of the judgment; and whosoever shall say to his brother, Raca, shall be in danger of the council: but whosoever shall say, Thou fool, shall be in danger of hell fire."

Here we have Jesus prescribing a mixture of obsolete Jewish laws and a surfeit of symbols. Strict compliance with those Jewish laws has been cast aside long ago. The word *Raca* means nothing to us today. It probably comes from the root *Reisch-Qof* which—in the Hebraic idiom— refers to saliva or spit. Did Jesus mean "who spits on his brother," or "you are a mouthful of spit," or what?

And what do we honestly make of prescriptions such as these that were given by Jesus: "If thy right eye offend thee, pluck it out," and, "If thy right hand offend thee, cut it off" (Matthew 5: 29, 30)? Do we know what he meant by the word *offend*? Was he led by the rabbinical style of his time? Or was he dead serious? If we adopt and keep an impartial attitude that is neither overcritical nor overcredulous, perhaps we shall understand what he meant in the last verse of that chapter: "Be ye therefore perfect, even as your Father which is in heaven is perfect" (Matthew 5:48).

Instead of trying endlessly to justify old customs of ages long past and gone (or hide them by publishing new expurgated versions ad nauseam), let us read with impartial discernment and extract what is essential. Let us not lose truth by deforming it in an effort to protect it.

The trick is to learn how to read these texts as the original writers intended them to be read. Today some of the most important words of the Bible are hopelessly misinterpreted and misunderstood. The original language of the text is in a code that has nothing to do with our so-called translations. For example, there is no "Father in heaven" in the original text. The word heaven is a mis-translation of *Shamaim*. According to the code, *Shamaim* is an equation that includes the cosmic life and the primal element of waters.

Another word that comes to mind is *sheep*, which is frequently attributed to Jesus to designate "one of his." Recently I was thinking how contemptible and repulsive that word is as a description of vital human beings. I was considering with what pleasure and delight Peter had adopted it in order to assert his personal authority. And I was saying to myself that if anyone—be he the Pope, the Father, the Son, and the Holy Ghost in one—called me a lamb, I would reply to such an insult to my humanity by bleating, *Baaaa*, and thus end our dialogue and relationship.

I recently received a form letter from a parish in Switzerland. Here are some extracts, translated from the French:

MESSAGE FROM OUR LORD
JESUS CHRIST TO THE WORLD

My sheep, I am come in my love to bring you back into the fold. You know that now times are grave, very grave. You see that . . . ALL this that was your world of false security is collapsing . . . but, Woe unto you! MADMEN! . . . You are preparing for yourselves AN ETERNITY OF PUNISH-MENT! You who DARE DEFY MY TEACHING AND THOSE OF MY CHURCH! . . . You will not defy THE FIRE OF ETERNAL DAMNATION! . . . You will not escape the terrible ETERNAL PUN-ISHMENT.

Then followed the classic grinding of teeth and the tears and the contrition with, finally, the address of that parish in Switzerland. I felt sad that that dirty sheet had been sent to me through people with whom I had previously had a courteous correspondence.

Fear is a disease, a contagious disease. Individuals would not propagate it unless they already had the disease themselves. The writers of that disgraceful document were certainly very sick and calling for help. This was a last-minute SOS, sent by people who felt their world and their security were already shattered.

And how could it not be so? Those who declare them-selves servants to the master and occupants of his dwelling during his absence (or supposed absence) have but two alternatives when his return is heralded: either to leave the place (which they do not do) or to declare that this is not he (which they are set on doing). And doing it, they are whirled at terrific speed into the remotest past.

I often meditate on the notion of "past" and on the jump that one can make beyond historical past—up to "the origin," which is the *now* of today. Historical time has no more reality than space or "matter." Historical time is a fabrication of our state of consciousness. The "Second Coming" is a psychological happening. It is possible at any moment because it is a constant presence—and certainly not an arrival at a prearranged hour in some airport who knows where!

The strangest aspect of this story is that the worship of a rabbi, who lived in the time of Pontius Pilate, leads worshipers farther and farther away from the truth he incarnated. The display and splendor of the rituals built up by the alluvions of time project the professional performers of these rituals into the past, which is the opposite direction of the flow of time. That mitered character who is carried on his palanquin all around St. Peter's Square to the applause of immense crowds conjures up scenes from ancient Egypt and Babylon. Truly, that character is long dead from a "dead death."

There are two entirely different deaths. To die to oneself psychologically and to be *in* that Coming is the joy of finding oneself totally new, completely free of fear, and without the slightest notion of sin. That is one death—resurrection. To die psychologically because one has developed a consciousness based on mythical beliefs and then the myth dies is the other death. In that death, one feels murdered. In confusion, anguish, and fear, one sinks into an unfathomable abyss of despair.

So we discover two separate spheres: the sphere of being *in* Him (one with Him), and the sphere of being *for* Him, which is only a mental and emotional projection. Those who are in Him have no problems, once the threshold has been passed. Those who are for Him, especially those who make a profession of it, are really only for the image they have created of him. They are so dependent upon creeds, doctrines, ceremonies, and innumerable disciplines, that all this paraphernalia becomes far more important to their so-called Christian consciences than original, living Truth.

Truth is always new—and thus unknown—if one is not *in* it without any notion of being *for* it. By holding to set images and identifying their "Christian consciences" with them, those who claim to be for Him let themselves be carried away into the past—into a past without real life.

Chapter 5

ENTER THE NEW ERA

PLEASE DO NOT IMAGINE THAT I HAVE FORGOT-
ten to "light my lantern"—to define what I mean by the
"Second Coming" and the "Return of the Rabbi." First it
was necessary to write about dying to one's self, about the
death of one's psychological structures, or, as Matthew put
it, "Then said Jesus unto his disciples, If any man will come
after me, let him deny himself, and take up his cross, and
follow me" (Matthew 16:24). Perhaps no instruction by the
Rabbi has been more perverted by odd interpretations than
this one. Actually, it is the simple statement that the personal self is not true and must be dropped. If that self is
untrue, then any thinking from the standpoint of such a self
is false. And certainly the "Second Coming" cannot be
understood by or with such false thinking.

This "Return of the Rabbi" does not subscribe to anything that one can think about. There is nothing in it to
understand, in the customary sense of that word. So, even
if those who have been willing to follow me this far have
not yet, in one click, created a void or emptiness in themselves, at least they have been made aware of it. For there
is nothing here to "understand."

To understand generally involves linking that which is
not understood to something we already know. Therefore,
such understanding is never new: it requires a link to the
old. If we do not find any link, that which is not understood remains not understood. If, for example, I speak of
tachyons, those unacquainted with the meaning of that
word do not understand what I am referring to. But if I

explain that tachyons are elements whose speed is superior to that of light, I have offered certain links, and they say that they understand. Therefore, such understanding is not new: it is simply a link to the old. And what has been really understood? Nothing. The words *elements, speed* and *light* are familiar, but what do they really mean? What, for instance, is light? The poor listener has merely stuffed tachyons into the same mysterious box with elements, speed, and light, and says that he or she understands what tachyons are.

So goes the world, confused in misunderstandings. And my words—"the Second Coming"—are as deceiving as the rest if you imagine that you have understood them. You have merely exchanged them for your pet ideas, accepting or rejecting them but not knowing what fact they are meant to identify.

Briefly the "Second Coming" or "Return of the Rabbi" is the irruption and deep penetration into our space-time consciousness of energies coming from an indeterminate number of universes having an indeterminate number of dimensions. Perhaps you will say that that is a very difficult definition for the "poor in spirit," or simple in mind. But let us not confuse the simple in mind with the simple-minded. The simple in mind is one who, having traversed all the complicated journeys of the human mind, has passed beyond them and has reached a new state—that of true maturity in which the indecomposable Essence has come to light.

Thus: "Blessed are the poor in spirit; for their's is the kingdom of heaven" (Matthew 5:3). Traditionalists who define the poor in spirit as the piously humble and submissive present a meaning that is absurd and untrue. The Rabbi who stated that the spirit is poor saw that it is simply not in the business of piling up material riches and possessions. It is outside the subject of money—way beyond it! Is that clear? And let us not misunderstand this: the simplest matter can be the most difficult to understand if our minds are confused and constipated with self-created problems indigenous only to our fictitious space-time continuum.

When I say that the "Second Coming" is taking place at this moment, I am frequently surprised—happily surprised—to receive a simple, affirmative response as though that fact is obvious. And maybe it is obvious. Perhaps I am only writing what many people already feel in the deepest recesses of the mind and heart. "The Return of Reb YHSHWH" has already begun. The very saying of it is charged with an explosive power sufficient to produce immediate effect. "The Return of Reb YHSHWH" has already begun. The understanding of it opens the New Era. "The Return of Reb YHSHWH" has already begun. The living of it inaugurates the era of the Spirit of Truth, and its light springs forth from the ruins of structures that have hidden it.

Chapter 6

ALL IS CONSCIOUSNESS

CONTRARY TO THE OPINIONS OF MANY SCIEN-tists, it is not the physical universe that produces consciousness; it is consciousness that produces the universe. A being coming from a universe of "n" dimensions would pass through our stone walls, steel buildings, and strongest armor without even seeing them—and without being seen by us. We know as a matter of fact that every external appearance is a void of vacuum in motion. This motion is a potential energy derived from two poles that neutralize each other statically. And this is what we call "matter," a word that makes no sense.

Today we have begun to accept what was said seventy-five years ago by such advanced thinkers as Jagadis Chandre Bose—that everything, absolutely everything, has consciousness of a sort—even metals. Recent experiments with plants indicate that plants react to our feelings and mental attitudes toward them.[1] If we learn how, we can communicate with them.

Passing from microcosm to macrocosm, the world has even become less inclined to laugh at astrology. The planets may have an influence on us. Centuries ago we accepted the idea that the Moon affects our ocean tides. If the Moon affects the waters of the sea, why shouldn't it affect our personal bodies, which are acknowledged to be 90 per-

---

[1]Peter Tompkins and Christopher Bird, *The Secret Life of Plants* (New York: HarperCollins, 1989).

cent water? And since we say that we are psychosomatic beings, why shouldn't the Moon thereby be affecting our psyches? *Psyche* means mind. Ergo, there exists a transmission of consciousness between the Moon and ourselves. And why shouldn't this hold true in our relationships with planets and other celestial bodies?

All of these phenomena—that is, the seeing, feeling, and living of what I have been writing—are part of the "Return of the Rabbi." By projecting into our human, earthly psyches a consciousness that belongs to worlds having an indeterminate number of dimensions, he taught and demonstrated that *in consciousness there are no insulated compartments—no partitions or dividing walls!* The Rabbi called Jesus declared himself to be *one* with his "Father" (universal consciousness), *one* with the lowest among us (Matthew 25:40), and *one* with Nature (the bread—his flesh; the wine—his blood).

Now let me come back to what I wrote earlier about the materialization of symbols, because I want to emphasize and explain something that is little understood. The fundamental error of these practices is common to all religions and their disciplines for attaining the divine. The breakthroughs that occur at times in certain psyches thrust energies into the symbols that come from worlds not conditioned by our space-time dimensions. Unfortunately they are always, *always*, translated into words that miss their true meaning and have no real significance—and into solid, material, and symbolic shapes indigenous to our world of relativity.

If that were the sole error, it would be only half-bad. Far worse—for all the religions based upon these breakthroughs by certain psyches into extraspace-time energies—is the fact that the churches then go on to structure their creeds not on the psychological devastation provoked by these breakthroughs, but (quite the reverse!) on desperate resistance to them—resistance to the inflow that would disrupt their old structures. Hence, instead of allowing themselves to become free of old structures, the psyches build walls of protection around them and project the would-be Revelation into a faraway heaven in a far-off future. The evolution becomes involution. The flying ahead becomes a creeping backward. That is the snare in which so many so-called religious devotees are caught. We shall see more of this later on when we examine the experiences of Paul and especially Peter.

Obviously it is not possible to condense a comparative study of all of the world's religions into one sentence. However, we can note that the religion resulting from the life, death, and teaching of the Rabbi called Jesus (whether historical or mythical) is unique. It is the only one that—far from offering a peaceful, appeasing mythology—plunges the psyche into a contradiction that seems unsolvable and also inflicts a terrible wound that cannot be healed.

In this book we shall not be discussing primitive religions based upon Earth forces and Earth worship. Such religions have been created by and for those who have not yet discovered their individuality. Their psyches meld into group souls of animal origin. Their religions link them to the past of their subspecies. Their vitality is fed by forces reflected from the Earth and not by the Cosmic Energy received directly by a person. They are still embryonic. And let us pass quickly over the fact that today many of our young people are seeking refuge in the soil. Caught in the anguish and confusion brought about by the end of a certain "world," they hope to find a religion by going back to the Earth.

Now we come to another refuge of the psyche—the myth. The mythical operation consists of sending back o the heavens—in the form of images—what the heavens have sent to us in the form of energy. The more the image resembles its true structure of cosmic energy, the more detached it is from the things of our world. And the more detached it is from our worldly things, the more solid, stable, durable, and indestructible it becomes.

For example, one immediately thinks of the Vedanta, those sublime texts that contain every truth: the cosmic forces, their inner contradictions, their apparent conflicts, their union, their wedding, the marvelous game of the immeasurable All. And this great All falls on this planet in an extravagant array of gods, goddesses, temples, sculptures, innumerable objects of worship, endlessly repeated prayers, mantras, meditations, ashrams, swamis, gurus, et cetera. In a rigid social classification strictly defined at the beginning, huge masses of people—hands folded in worship, minds longing for an immovable state of felicitous being—await the revolutions from outside that will overthrow their entire world, materially and psychologically. To our knowledge, only the Rabbi has projected into psyches in an irremediable way this cosmic play of contradictory energies. Mad with grief and sorrow after his disappearance, how could such psyches have taken refuge in the deceitful shelter of a fabricated myth?

Paul was the first to feel the necessity of freeing himself from the security given by obedience to the Law of the Torah. He failed, we know. His rabbinical conditioning made him stumble at every step. Hence his perpetual nightmare: sin—the sin into which he plunged the Church. I shall come back to that later: sin is not the subject of this chapter. My immediate aim is to offer my contribution to what the most advanced scientific minds are discovering today: a new perspective of consciousness or, rather, a sphere of consciousness that includes all that is—from stones to galaxies to all the in-betweens, including plants, animals, fish, birds, humans, plus all that is beyond our perception and understanding, gods and, if you will, God.

The old separation of earth and heaven has disappeared. I say that this new perception is part of the "Second Coming" or "Return of the Rabbi." I cannot put it more clearly than to repeat: *In consciousness there are no insulated compartments—no partitions or dividing walls!* And I also want to repeat that there is a coexistence and interpenetration of an indeterminate number of universes of indeterminate dimensions. Every one of these universes is the projection of a particular state of consciousness. The sum total of these states of consciousness constitutes the universal consciousness—God, if you prefer that word, but only on the condition that you give it no "thinkable" definition.

Our real self—the very essence of our individuality since in consciousness there are no insulated compartments, partitions, or dividing wals—is located without any separations in the totality of this universal phenomenon that is the life of the Universe. Our true self is our multidimensional soul. But we, as we appear in our physical bodies, are only temporary emanations of our true self, our multidimensional soul. Such is the teaching of Reb YHSHWH, expressed by one of his, according to his ability in the words of today.

Chapter 7

A TEACHING?

HIS TEACHING? WHAT DO WE REALLY KNOW OF it? Almost nothing. Ask around. Ask your friends and neighbors. Carry out a survey in your city or town. Ask the preachers, teachers, politicians, businesspeople, union officials, and socially elite.

Go even further. Inquire in every place where the shadow of the Cross weighs down people's souls with that corpse smeared with blood. And from all your asking, you will gather little or nothing, or dreams and imagination.

Who is this Rabbi called Jesus?

"God." God, despite his apostles' testimony. "For there is one God, and one mediator between God and man, the man Christ Jesus" (I Timothy 2:5). Is that clear? And that quotation is taken at random, just by opening the Bible casually. There are many such examples in the New Testament.

The Rabbi was deified in spite of himself. It would have been scandalous, foolhardy, and fatal for a rabbi to call himself God. Instead, the Rabbi identifies himself time after time as Ben-Adam, which has been erroneously translated as "son of man." We shall explain such terms as Ben-Adam later. He does not usurp for himself alone the status of "Son of God." He declares explicitly that his "sonship" is accessible to us all and invites us to "be ye therefore perfect even as your Father is perfect." He exhorts, "do not call 'father' your father according to the flesh, but he who is in Shamaim." Unfortunately this passage from Matthew 23:9 has been translated in the English version as, "And call no man your father upon the earth: for one is your Father, which is in heaven." *Shamaim* should not be translated as "heaven," as we shall see later.

Paul, whose mind is at times quite subtle, makes a clear distinction on the subject: "For in him dwelleth all the fulness of the Godhead bodily. And ye are complete in him, which is the head of all principality and power" (Colossians 2: 9,10).

That is an obvious statement, if you remember what I have tried to say and am still trying to say: that the Cosmic Consciousness is *in us*. The Rabbi was aware of it. Some of us are not. As he was aware of it, he radiated it. Those of us who are not aware of it emit darkness.

Paul writes again in Philippians 3:15, "Let us therefore, as many as be perfect, be thus minded." We must restore the word *perfect* to its proper meaning. What does Paul mean? What does this word mean to me? And, going further, what does Reb YHSHWH (the Rabbi called Jesus) mean to me?

Here is somebody who is said to have died on a cross and to have risen from the dead in resurrection—but so secretly that even his mother and disciples failed to recognize him, and so surreptitiously that his resurrection lasted only forty days. In that supposed state of resurrection, he passed through closed doors and never allowed anyone to touch him. After Thomas told the disciples that he would not believe until he could "put [his] finger into the print of the nails and thrust [his] hand into his side" (St. John 20:25), the Rabbi reappears and tells Thomas to do so. Thomas believes—and does not touch him.

The Rabbi was obviously in an "astral body." Or, rather, he who came was his "double." In this respect, let me call attention to a passage in *Tales of Power* by Carlos Castaneda.[1] Don Genaro explains how he materialized and

---

[1]Carlos Castaneda, *Tales of Power* (New York: Pocket Books, 1984).

gave life to his double while dreaming it in his sleep. This double is himself—but in a subtle body. when he meets Castaneda in that body, Castaneda tries to touch him, but cannot, because an invisible obstacle acts as a protection to that body. Does this help to explain the Rabbi's appearance after his supposed death—an event that we are not at all sure of?

What is the Rabbi? He gave birth to a new era that has filled twenty centuries of history so far, but the people of his time did not really see or know him. Was he the mysterious Master of Wisdom of the Essenes? Was he a revolutionary radical? Or was he an unsuccessful commander-in-chief Messiah of a Jewish army? And what is the Rabbi to me that I am compelled to write what I am writing—against my own will?

And what am I writing? This is not a treatise on Jesus Christ. It could be called an epistle to my known and unknown friends and enemies. Or perhaps a testament—quite proper at my age of 83. Or maybe a gospel for the new age. (Pardon me for entering into such personal matters. I feel that if I can clarify what he—my Master and my Self—is for me, I can perhaps help some of my readers discover if and how he is something to them.) To me, he is not the son of a virgin made pregnant by some new edition of Jupiter pursuing his amorous adventures this time in the shape of a dove. Nor is he, in his nature, essentially different from any of us.

Can we translate into our modern understanding these words of Paul: "God, to them who are the called . . . . he also did predestinate to be conformed to the image of his Son, that he might be the firstborn among many brethren" (Romans 8:28,29)? The word *firstborn* rings some ancient bells. "And thou shalt say unto Pharaoh, Thus saith the Lord, Israel is my son, even my firstborn" (Exodus 4:22). "I am a father to Israel, and Ephraim is my firstborn" (Jeremiah 31:9). So a deity called God declares that his firstborn son is Israel, and apparently Israel appeared at least three times in the flesh: first, with Jacob, who acquired that name ("Thy name shall be called no more Jacob, but Israel" [Genesis 32:28]) after his famous wrestle with the man or angel or God ("And Jacob called the name of the place Peniel: for I have see God face to face, and my life is preserved" [Genesis 32:30]); second, with Ephraim; and third, with the Rabbi. Who is this deity? In Exodus 6:2,3 we read, "And God spake unto Moses, and said unto him, I am the Lord: And I appeared unto Abraham, unto Isaac, and unto Jacob, by the name of God Almighty, but by my name JE-HO-VAH was I not known to them."

I must intervene vehemently here! That name JE-HO-VAH is spelled Yod-Hay-Waw-Hay in Hebrew. It is an equation that has a very definite meaning. I have gone into it in great detail in other books so will simply state the sense and significance of it here: Israel, hence the Rabbi, is the explosive germ contained in the hard shell structured by Moses, the Jews, and their Law. In terms of Cosmic Consciousness, this double life is an inherent timelessness projected into time as containers (bodies). The One Life acquires awareness of itself through the interplay of its two exponents and, historically, always appears as a conflict. "And Simeon blessed them, and said unto Mary . . . behold, this child is set for the fall and rising again of many in Israel; and for a sign which shall be spoken against" (Luke 2:34). From beginning to end, the Bible is the story of this conflict. It appears as the struggle between two "brothers" or between two "sons," with the persistent assertion that the "elder" is engendered by the explosive energy.

So now I know what the Rabbi is to me, because I know what he is and what I am—akin in the explosive side of the Cosmic Energy. Historically, this means a state of contradiction, a denial of tradition, worship, and every structure that is not of the explosive component of Life.

And I know that I am of those described in Acts 28:22 as "everywhere . . . spoken against."

This Second Coming happens indeed at a time when the contradictions are such that this world can no longer live. The contradiction must be accomplished. It must come to its dramatic end, as happened 2,000 years ago for a world that was in the process of being destroyed. Again the Scriptures must be fulfilled by the irruption of the living contradiction in psyches petrified in deadlock. This irruption is in me, as it was in me at the time of Pontius Pilate. This inner movement of all consciousness, this necessary duality in the Cosmic energy as it projects itself into the conflicts of humanity—in a word, Israel—is come again. Israel incarnate—the Rabbi.

So here am I, almost exhausted at 83 but forced to climb out of my comfortable bomb shelter and expose myself by writing these words. What is this self that bears my name, and who is this "I" with which I never asked to be identified? Indeed, I am Jonah. I have always fled, never wanting to obey the inner voice. And if I am now led to adopt a personal tone in writing these pages, it is because my soul has caught me up. This soul is my multidimensional individuality living a state of consciousness with no insulated compartments, partitions, or dividing walls—living in multiple universes that coexist with and penetrate our limited universe.

My soul, of which the man bearing my name is but one of its emanations appearing in history's apparent reality, shot its divine poisonous ray into me fifty years ago. Then followed fifty years of meetings and separations, imprisonments and escapes, and victories and defeats worthy of St. John of the Cross and (if humor still has its place) of a good western or murder mystery.

Sometimes I wish that I could write in the manner of Paul: "I, Suarès, a servant of X, Y, Z, called to be an apostle, exhort you, my brethren, to announce Aleh, Beth, Gimel."

It might be an easy matter if I had had extraordinary visions and believed in them. But, alas, I am compelled (I don't know by whom) to expose myself simply because I have nothing to lose. Had an imperative voice from heaven or hell spoken to me, my words might not be questioned. I could have repeated its commands with authority and proclaimed myself a teacher. Many people do that these days, and it is the fashion to follow them no matter what they say or don't say. But I have only my critical judgment to go by, and I notice almost every moment of my life how difficult it is to be intelligent.

In thinking of the visions that I have never had, I remember what the "Virgin" is said to have declared during the appearances of that idol in the image of her iconographies: "Pray me! Pray me!" That repeated entreaty said clearly that gods who are not prayed to lose stature and deflate like a leaking balloon.

I think also how Teresa of Avila maltreated her body to the point of destroying its sensations. Feelings, however, must find a way to express themselves. One day while crossing a vestibule she became so filled with horror at the sight of a statue of Christ tortured on his cross and dripping with blood (in the best Spanish realism) that that Christ came and settled on her left shoulder. Thereafter he gave her directions for all of her actions. Or did she give them to herself through that projection?

I have never played such tricks on myself. My "conscious consciousness," as some people call it, had suffered from suffocation as far back as I can remember in a world that was totally incomprehensible to me.

"Mom, how does the grass grow?'

"My child, it is made to grow by God."

"Oh, I see."

Children ask many questions and are frequently satisfied with any answer they receive. I never asked anything because all of existence was incomprehensible to me. But I knew, as a very small child, that I had been in jail. I had the feeling of it. Gradually as I grew up, everything that I knew and met—family, cities, countryside, sun, sky, and stars—surrounded me with their impenetrability.

Then one day I received a blow right in my solar plexus: it said that for ever and ever and ever my consciousness was imprisoned in the universe. However vast and glorious it is, *I would never know how it is that anything at all exists*. That is when I "lost my life"—that is, my psychological structures. Such vital disasters never happen through prayers, meditations, or disciplines. They are death blows.

When a new and very delicate new Life was born in my heart, I knew what it was.

Much later I happened to read a book about young Martin Luther and his life up to the time that he nailed his ninety-five theses onto the church door in Wittenberg. What he became later is irrelevant. The book described his character as a young man. According to the author, Luther had two chief characteristics: he could not accept the evidence of his sensory world, and he was desperately in search of his true individuality. The two characteristics were exactly my own.

At the beginning of this chapter, I wrote that we know almost nothing of the teaching of the Rabbi. Could it be that there *is* no teaching—that, after all is said and done, it is but a question of maturing?

Chapter 8

FULFILL THE SCRIPTURES

"FULFILL THE SCRIPTURES." OF COURSE, THAT IS a matter of ripening, of maturing. But what exactly do those words mean?

Can we jump into the mutation demanded by our time? If the mutation is not in us, what unknown direction shall we take in order to find it? Must we just follow our usual tendencies and hope that they lead to the source? What is the source for those of us who are steeped in the Judeo-Christian myth? What is revelation? Most of us have a sense of having lost something. But what?

And why do I write that the source is Israel and that the Rabbi is Israel? How do I know? What is Israel? And what did the Rabbi teach that we do not know or do not want to know? "And he taught in their synagogues, being glorified of all" (Luke 4:15). Would any man have been permitted to teach in a synagogue if he were not a rabbi?

In the same chapter, Luke relates the scandal caused by the Rabbi when, on the Sabbath, he entered the synagogue "as his custom was" and read aloud from the book of Isaiah: "The Spirit of the Lord is upon me . . . . to preach the acceptable year of the Lord. And he closed the book and began to say unto them, This day is this scripture fulfilled in your ears" (Luke 4: 16-21). His words provoked instant upheaval. He was attacked, cast out of the city, and barely escaped being thrown over a cliff.

"This day is this scripture fulfilled in your ears." When we understand what he meant by fulfillment of this scripture, then we are in him and we no longer search for the

Origin, or the Source, or the Revelation, or whatever name you care to give it.

Today we know that the Gospels are mythological narratives, not historical documents. But that does not justify those who deliberately present a perverted picture of the Rabbi that contradicts the Bible stories. Many learned Catholics become upset when I point out that Jesus was a Jew. One of my purposes in this world is to remind both Christians and Jews of this fact. The Christians have perverted the picture of Jesus to the point of making him unrecognizable. The Jews have refused to recognize him at all—and have been murdered for it. Every word of the Bible was written by Jews, with the exception of the Gospel according to Luke. Luke was a Greek doctor and a close friend of Paul, who influenced him. The Old and New Testaments are one book, even though many churches insist on separating them.

Today going back to the sources has become the fashion, just as it was fashionable for upper-class Victorians to take the waters a century ago. Where are you going this summer? I'm going back to the sources. And the result is similar to the Franciscan scholar I mentioned earlier. There are many other curiosity shops—the Dead Sea Scrolls, the Rosicrucians, the Order of Malta, the Templars, the Cathars, the alchemists, the occultists, the cabalists, the convoys of swamis in their Rolls Royces—need I go on?

In the last few years we have had at least three or four new translations of the Bible. They are all on the same model, repeating the same old errors. Scholars may have worked a lifetime over each of them, but they have not allowed a new state of consciousness to penetrate them. Frequently I am asked, "If that is so and if you are so set on the new, why are you always up to your neck in this old Bible?" The answer is simple: because I am the living germ inside it, and you are trying to murder me. Since you cannot succeed because I am immortal and since all your efforts are murdering *you*, I blow up.

Many institutions, including the Soviets, have tried to pull down religion from the outside. They have succeeded only in strengthening it. I have no intention of destroying what is called religion. That which must explode is the distance you are putting between the Revelation and yourselves.

You consider Adam, Eve, Cain, Abel, and others to have lived in the past. That is not so. They never existed in the past, but they are perfectly alive inside you—and they are doing exactly the opposite of what you believe they did. You call Elohim "God" and YHWH (that's how I spell it) "the Lord." No God and no Lord were ever meant to appear "out there." The energies that are expressed in the original equations now mis-translated as Elohim and YHWH are inside you—but almost dead from the beatings you give them. But now we have reached a point where there is no choice. You are condemned to live joyfully in the explosive fulfillment of everything that you have previously distorted in your vain efforts to "believe" instead of to "know."

What can I do about those old and new Scriptures that for 5,000 and 2,000 years have been read and read and read, and that have been counterfeited in every idiom by space-time minds that materialize their own erroneous projections in vain efforts to climb imaginary stairs to heaven? What use have we of this so-called monotheism of which Jews and Christians are so proud? In almost every case, it worships a multifarious deity who frequently serves as nothing but a war apparatus.

Then must we reject the Bible wholesale? Far from it! Let us get back to work and correct the job that we did so badly 2,000 years ago, realizing that "2,000 years ago" is here now because linear time does not really exist. We, who were and are companions of the Rabbi, will achieve what we began. He gave us the key that opens all the secret doors to the original Revelation. Some of us did not grasp the key. Others lost it. Those who used it could open the doors only halfway.

"Then came the darkness of centuries." And one morning a few years ago I woke up and found that I had the key! To have it was not enough: I had to learn it, and I had to learn to use it. But there was nothing to help me— not one document among the billions of accumulated manuscripts. There was not even a hint, no matter how distorted. Still, I knew that what I had received was indeed a key, and that he who had handed it to me was the Rabbi, the Master of Masters.

For some years I fumbled with it as best I could. It did open up the Scriptures. It did enlarge my vision and understanding. Yet I felt uncertain about it. Did I know or did I merely imagine that it had come from the Rabbi? I tried to persuade myself that it didn't matter where it came from, as long as it worked. But I needed something to relieve my uncertainty.

Then one day a friend brought me a book: *Apocryphal Gospels, Acts and Revelations*, Volume XVI, Edinburgh, T. & T. Clark, 38 George Street, 1870. Obviously, one must be very cautious with Apocrypha. They are mostly popular legends recorded long after the happenings they relate. Usually the apocryphal works copy each other. They repeat little stories bubbling over with miracles upon miracles, and are intended to rouse the faith of naive people. Such tales were originally transmitted orally and repeated with some variations. Typical is the story of the birds that Jesus sculpted from clay. He breathed upon them, and they flew away.

Many such documents report that the Rabbi knew everything that there is to know, from alpha to omega. They all mention the Greek alphabet, an indication that they are far from genuine, far from the original setting. But here is an extract of what I read in the volume that my friend brought me:

An Arabic Gospel of the Savior's Infancy

There was, moreover, at Jerusalem a certain man named Zacheus, who taught boys. He said to Joseph, "Why, O Joseph, dost thou not bring Jesus to me to learn his letters?" Joseph agreed to do so, and reported the matter to Lady Mary. They therefore took Him to the master; he, as soon as he saw Him, wrote out the alphabet for Him, and told him to say *Aleph*. And when he had said *Aleph*, the master ordered him to pronounce *Beth*. And the Lord Jesus said to him, "Tell me first the meaning of *Aleph*, and then I will pronounce *Beth*." And when the master threatened to flog him, the Lord Jesus explained to him the meaning of the letters *Aleph* and *Beth*; also which figures of the letters were straight, which crooked, which drawn round into a spiral, which marked with points, which without them, why one letter went before another; and many other things He began to recount and elucidate which the master himself had never either heard or read in any book. The Lord Jesus moreover, said to the master: "Listen, and I shall say them to thee." And he began clearly and distinctly to repeat Aleph, Beth, Gimel, Daleth, on to Taw. And the master was astonished, and said: "I think that this boy was born before us all." And turning to Joseph, he said: "Thou hast brought to me to be taught a boy more learned than all the masters." To the Lady Mary also he said: "This son of thine has no need of instruction." Thereafter they took him to another and more learned master, who, when he saw him, said: "Say *Aleph*."[1]

---

[1]Modern readers will find this discussion on page 57 of *The Lost Books of the Bible and the Forgotten Books of Eden* (New York: Meridian, 1963).

Then follows a repetition of that story except that this time the master flogged Him, and immediately the master's hand dried up and he died. The same story is again repeated, adding that when Jesus was 12, he taught the teachers and their chief, who declared: "Hitherto I have neither attained to nor heard of such knowledge."

No matter whether Jesus was 7 or 12 or older, those statements must be considered very seriously. What could the alphabet reveal that no learned teacher knew? In our Western schools, no teacher or student would demand, "Tell me the meaning of the letter *A*." Nobody would be called upon to explain why one letter goes before another in our alphabet. And what was it that a gathering of the most learned Jews did not know when they most certainly had studied everything concerning their religion? What could be the knowledge hidden in the alphabet that they had never heard of?

The answers are clear. That alphabet is a code of tremendous importance. The Hebrew letters and numbers constitute an immense explanation of Cosmic Energy and consciousness. I have been writing it and saying it for years. I have showed it to learned rabbis who know nothing of it and who still read the Bible in idiomatic Hebrew. And, a fortiori, need I mention the misinterpretations of the Bible in all the other languages?

At this point a friend commented that when Jesus said, "I will not pronounce Beth," he pronounced it. That is not necessarily so. One can say Aleph, Beth, and all the other letters without pronouncing them so as to give them their power. The same is true for every sound or articulation belonging to the original code. This is particularly the case with YHWH. You can say YHWH over and over again, but it will not be It. And those who know It are very few indeed.

For me, the authenticity of the apocryphal legend that I have quoted is not important. What is important is its indication that a secret and all-embracing science is hidden in the Hebrew alphabet. And that secret, all-embracing science is, I discovered, a fact!

All through the centuries there have been cabalists who studied that science. But so far as I know, none of them has suspected that it contradicted their way of reading the Bible. Evidently the times were not ripe for the discovery that the first five chapters of Genesis—when read with the knowledge of the original code ("tell me first the meaning of Aleph")—are a treatise on Cosmic Energy considered both objectively and subjectively in terms of consciousness. These chapters describe, in a language that has no grammar, the process of consciousness as it projects itself in forms and as it becomes aware of itself by separating itself from its projections.

Modern science is beginning to catch up with this knowledge. Five thousand and two thousand years of Bible interpretation must inevitably be overturned. The inner core of the Scriptures must be fulfilled. And the only way to discover that inner core is by reading the Scriptures as they were meant to be read. I have been clamoring for such a drastic revision. I have given the key to it. The Second Coming is now opening a number of psyches. The call is beginning to be heard.

Chapter 9

⁓

WHO DO WE LEARN FROM?

FREQUENTLY I FEEL IT NECESSARY TO REPEAT myself, not only in books dealing with this subject but also in everything else that I write—and almost on every page. No doubt it is because of the nature of my subject matter. What I am attempting to do is equivalent to trying to describe the world to an unborn baby. How can people hear or understand me from their upside-down position inside the womb of old religious organizations that promote rituals, prayers, confessions, and disciplines? It is not surprising that those who consider themselves already righteous do not even care to listen.

What are the strange psychological barriers blocking the path for both Jews and Christians to the simple understanding that the Rabbi, in the body he had taken at that time, was a rabbi and the Master of Cabala—that is, the Incarnation of Israel? Many ask what proof I have for these assertions. I reply that the Cabala is the knowledge of the manifested and unmanifested living Cosmic Energy—God, if you insist on that word—and that that knowledge is contained and easily discovered in the signs constituting the Hebrew alphabet.

Then they want to know why I declare that the Rabbi's thoughts were based upon the Cabala when no existing document reports that to be so. Well, let me point to an example in the Gospels—an example that is extremely important, decisive, and absolute. It is a word, only one word. But it says everything and explains everything. It explains what the Rabbi is, what the Church of Peter is, and

2,000 years of theology and doctrines that try to evade the issue, to forget that word and to hide it from Peter's "sheep." One word, a single word. The Rabbi must have intervened personally in order to have it still there in Gospels that have suffered so many alterations and interpolations over the centuries. That one single word, addressed to Peter at Caesarea Philippi by the Rabbi called Jesus: *Satan!*"

You will find it in Matthew 16:23: "But he turned, and said unto Peter, Get thee behind me, Satan: thou art an offence unto me: for thou savourest not the things that be of God, but those that be of men."

In my vocabulary, Peter's consciousness is blocked in our space-time continuum and is not open to the Rabbi's multidimensional universes.

The word *Satan* is a very ancient Hebrew word, pronounced "Sah-tahn." It has a very definite cabalistic meaning. Or, more accurately, it is an equation, the meaning of which varies according to the variations of the schemata that constitute it. I have explained the word *Satan* many times in many lectures and writings. But I am not among those who make themselves heard in the right places and who are listened to as "authorities." The stupid, mad meaning that some "authorities" give to the word *Satan* forces them to avoid mentioning the passage in Matthew that I have just quoted. This passage is especially embarrassing to them because it comes so soon after the Rabbi's statement to Peter in Matthew 16:19, "And I will give unto thee the keys of the kingdom of heaven." In other words (their words), the Rabbi apparently gives the keys of the kingdom of heaven to the master of hell!

The Rabbi has already told the disciple, "And I also say unto thee, That thou are Peter, and upon this rock I will build my church" (Matthew 16:18). So the Catholic Church that Peter founded is Satan's church. Is that it?

For heaven or hell's sake, let's not indulge in such nonsense. And I suggest that the only way out of such nonsense is the understanding of the code. So once again I shall give it—briefly and just enough of it so that one can understand what the Rabbi really meant. The code is vitally important for the fulfillment of the Scriptures and, generally speaking, for the "full-filling" of our churches and synagogues. More vital still, the code can lead us out of a nightmare in which God and Satan, good and evil, the divine and the carnal, fight in vain the endless contradictions of consciousness split in two.

Many people object when I suggest that they learn the Hebrew letters and the code. They find various excuses. Some people complain that such study is difficult and takes time. And will anything really come from it? they ask. "The proof of the pudding is in the eating," I reply, in my best British accent, and move on.

Actually, the code is easy to grasp. The difficulty lies in our psyches. They resist the truth and fight for their own so-called lives. Many people cannot accept the code because it is not presented by a celebrated "authority." "Who is behind all this?" an authority worshiper asked me. "Who taught you?"

"I learned it from Reb Schmouel ben Yehoudah from Bialystok," I replied.

"And from whom did he get it?" asked my questioner.

"From Reb Yaakov ben Hamenorah of Kielce," I said.

"And from whom . . ." began my friend, then stopped because he saw that I was pulling his leg.

To whom, by whom, from whom—that is the story of the authority worshipers. I predict that some of them will soon carry their lines of authority back far enough to reach the anthropoids or the primal living cell. Fortunately, most such people are still satisfied to stop at the authority they happen to approve of at the moment. "Thus spake

Zarathustra, Plato, or Simeon ben Yoahi." If the right voice said it, the followers then feel justified in not bothering to think for themselves.

Another example: recently a well-known philosophy professor asked me if I would care to deliver a talk to his students. I said that I would, and gave him a brief outline of what I might say. On a pad I wrote the meanings of the letter-numbers: *Aleph* (1), *Bayt* (2), *Ghimel* (3), *Dalleth* (4). I didn't go further because four is a structure, or whole. Four can be the response to information (active resistance) or the refusal of it (passive resistance). In this latter case, it is symbolized by a square, which is apparently solid but has no real resistance (as a triangle has). In the Bible, four is associated with the power of the kings. As an example, I mentioned that Judah, who gave birth to a royal line of kings, was Jacob's fourth son.

"I accept your explanations of numbers 1, 2, and 3 because they are in Plato," said the authority-loving professor. Then he roared, "But Judah *could* have been other than Jacob's fourth son."

His words made me dizzy. "He *was* his fourth son!" I shouted and ran away. So his pupils were not subjected to the martyrdom of listening to something that they did not already know.

But now, before meeting Jesus and Peter face to face in Caesarea Philippi again, I have positively made up my mind to subject my readers to an ordeal similar to the one that the professor's pupils escaped: I will lead you to the key to the Scriptures—the letter-numbers.

Chapter 10

~

THE LETTER-NUMBERS

AS A SIMPLE SERIES OF LETTERS, THIS ALPHABET is as easy to learn as the Greek alphabet or ours. In fact, we and the Greeks have imitated much of it. The Greek *Alpha, Beta, Gamma, Delta* is almost a repetition of the Hebrew *Aleph, Bayt, Ghimel, Dallet*. Our A, B, C, and D come close to it. Our K, L, M, and N match in order *Kaf, Lammed, Mem*, and *Noun*. And Q, R, S, and T appear as *Qof, Raysh, Seen*, and *Taw* in Hebrew. So twelve letters out of twenty-two are almost twins. I hope that you have breathed a sigh of relief and will never again say, "Hebrew? It's Chinese to me!" It is unfortunate that language instruction in many of our universities does not go farther back into history than the Greek alphabet. As a result, few people know how closely we are attached to the Semitic roots of the sacred language.

Now, for something a bit more complex—Hebrew has no numeric characters such as 1, 2, 3, and 4. Instead, every letter corresponds to a number. This does not seem so strange when we remember that Latin numbers are also letters: I, V, X, L, C, et cetera. The first nine letters in the Hebrew alphabet represent the first nine numbers. *Aleph* is 1, *Bayt* is 2, *Gimel* is 3, and so forth. the next nine letters run in "tens." *Yod* is 10, *Kaf* is 20, *Lammed* is 30, and so forth. Then the following four letters stand for hundreds. *Qof* is 100, *Raysh* is 200, *Seen* is 300, and *Tav* is 400. And to complete the alphabet, the final five letters run in hundreds from 500 to 900, but they change shape when they come at the end of a word.

Letter	Value	Letter	Value	Letter	Value
Aleph	1	Yod	10	Qof	100
Bayt (Vayt)	2	Kaf (Khaf)	20	Raysh	200
Ghimel (Djimel)	3	Lammed	30	Seen (Shaen)	300
Dallet (Thallet)	4	Mem	40	Tav (Thav)	400
Hay	5	Noun	50	Final Khaf	500
Vav (Waw)	6	Sammekh	60	Final Mem	600
Zayn	7	Ayn	70	Final Noun	700
Hhayt	8	Pay (Phay)	80	Final Phay	800
Tayt	9	Tsadde	90	Final Tsadde	900

Chart 1. The Letter-Numbers (Autiot).

The numerical values of the letters have psychological meanings of great importance in the sacred language. When one lives with them in this way, they give immediate information and feeling. They belong to both the mind and the heart, and unite them.

We, too, give psychological meanings to some numbers. For instance, there is our immediate happy reaction to the lucky number 11. At the other extreme, our number 13 conjures up such fear of bad luck that most American skyscrapers do not have a 13th floor. They skip from the 12th floor to the 14th floor without explanation.

But let's get back to the sacred language. Every number in it is considered a whole being and cannot be torn apart. For example, 6 is only 6; it cannot also be identified as 2 x 3. 7 is only 7; it is not also 3 + 4. And so forth.

The reverse is true for the letters. Every letter (except Hay, which stands for "life") is composed of two or three other letters that, in their turn, are composed of two or three letters. The result is an anatomical chart representing endless processes (See Chart 1; Aleph, Bayt, Yod). In other words, the letters do not merely stand for sounds. Each of them is a name—the name of an equation relating to one of the innumerable aspects of cosmic energy. And it is up to us to solve the equations.

This poses no problem to our scientific Western minds. We are used to equations. Take, for example, Albert Einstein's famous $E = mc^2$. We know that we can understand it only when we have learned what those letters, numbers, and symbols stand for. Unfortunately, the language of advanced mathematics requires years of study. Fortunately, the sacred language comes naturally to an understanding that is open to revelation.

With what the Cabala calls the three "mother letters"—*Aleph, Mem, Sheen*— we get an immediate picture of energy functioning in an equation that is quite similar to Einstein's theory. My American friends Bob Toben and

48 / *Carlo Suarès*

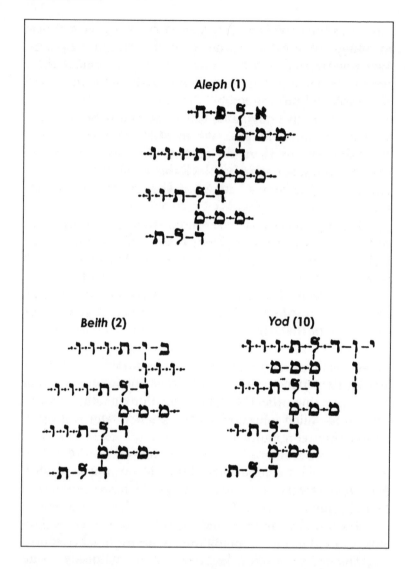

Chart 2. Anatomical charts of Aleph and of two letters that "Play the Game with it." For a complete survey of the Autiot, see The Spectograms of the Hebrew Alphabet *by Carlo Suarès translated into English by F. A. Wolf. Pub. note: We were not able to locate this book in English.*

physicists Fred Wolf and Jack Sarfatti have had no difficulty following me in the elaboration of that equation. Furthermore, this equation integrates the psychic energy, but Einstein's does not. And this scientific approach is far closer to being "in the Rabbi" than the study and worship of what religions imagine he was or is. The key is scientific. It is science at its best. We must stop imagining that "God spoke to Abraham in Hebrew." We must stop waving the Bible in the air and shouting ignorantly that this is the Word of God when we have not yet learned what it really says.

The alphabet is easy, the numbers are easy, and the code is easy. The only problem is how to free minds that insist on remaining in jail. Open your minds, for fulfillment is there.

The Aleph has always been the symbol of the greatest possible energy. In very ancient times it was drawn in the shape of a bull's head because the bull was, for those people, the embodiment of power. The symbol as it appears today has all of the attributes of a cross—but of a changeable, unattainable cross, symbol of a mysterious double life. Depending upon the state of our thinking, that double life can be called vibration and fluctuation, eternality and temporality, continuity and interruption, explosion and compression, et cetera. It is a totality in itself.

The *Bayt* is a double fertilization by *Waw*—one coming from *Tav*, the other from *Yod*. Both are included in the biological process.

The *Yod* is a variant of *Bayt*. It expresses the self-generation of existence, a perpetual repetition of prototypes.

The last letter of the alphabet is *Taw*. All that is exists between *Aleph* and *Taw*. *Tav* is *Aleph's* tabernacle or sanctuary. *Tav* is none other than *Aleph* itself in its compressive and fertile powers.

And now I shall give you the phonetic alphabet, a chart of the letter spellings and their relations to each other.

Vay	Hay	Dallet	Ghimel	Bayt	Aleph
וו	ח	דלת	גמל	בית	אלפ
Lammed	**Kaf**	**Yod**	**Tayt**	**Hhayt**	**Zayn**
למד	כפ	יוד	טית	חית	זין
Tsadde	**Phay**	**Ayn**	**Sammeth**	**Noun**	**Mem**
צרי	פח	עיג	ממכ	נון	ממ
		Tav	**Sheen**	**Raysh**	**Qof**
		תו	שין	ריש	קופ

Chart 3.   The Spellings.

The phonetic spellings in English are a matter of choice. For example, the letter that I call *Bayt* has been written by others as *Beyt, Beith, Beth*, et cetera. These variations are not important. Of more importance is the fact that the letter *Hay* is formulated *Hay-Aleph* by some and *Hay-Yod* by others. I disagree with both.

"I AM THAT I AM," the English version of the Moses revelation in Exodus 3:14, has been mis-translated with the addition of an extra "I AM" that doesn't belong there. "Ehiay Asher Ehiay," the original mis-translation, most certainly should be read: *Aleph-Hay-Yod-Hay*—Aleph living Yod living. *Hay* is conferred on both *Aleph* and *Yod*. In other words, the Eternal is alive and the Temporal is alive. It is, in a nutshell, a total Revelation in which all possible revelations are included.

Chapter 11

WHAT DOES THE ALEPH-BAYT MEAN?

HERE IS A VERY SIMPLIFIED EXPLANATION OF the letter-numbers:

1. *Aleph* is the supreme living Energy. It is One, but it is also hidden in multiplicity. Aleph is immeasurable. Its speed would therefore come under the mathematical symbol for "infinite."
2. *Bayt* is any support of *Aleph*. One of the postulates of the Cabala is: *Aleph* with everything, everything with *Aleph, Bayt* with everything, everything with *Bayt*. This means that the eternal is everywhere, in all that is, and that all is *Bayt*. The Hebrew definition of *Bayt* is: house, container, support of the eternal.
3. *Ghimel* is the archetype of all the movements that constitute the biological phenomena.
4. *Dallet* is any resistance, whether passive or active.
5. *Hay* is Life.
6. *Waw* is the male copulative element.
7. *Zayn* is the free Energy, the final element of "solution-dissolution."
8. *Hhayt* is the archetype of the primal Energy, unstructured and of the unconscious.
9. *Tayt* is every cell.

The tens are the existential projections of the letter-numbers 1 to 9 above.

10. *Yod* is the living, corporal, contradictory projection of Aleph (1).
20. *Kaf* is the action of *Bayt* (2), particularly in physical man.
30. *Lammed* is the organic movement controlled.
40. *Mem* is water, the primal element, where its opposite, *Dallet* (4), is born.
50. *Noun,* contrary to the infinite, boundless *Hay* (5), is life confined and conditioned in existence.
60. *Sammekh* is the female sex, opposite partner of *Waw* (6).
70. *Ayn,* which is not translatable phonetically, is the key to every freedom.
80. *Pay* is the *Hhayt* (8) in existence.
90. *Tsadde* is the symbol of all structure.

The hundreds are the cosmic projections of the first four archetypes.

100. *Qof* integrates the cosmic contradiction of *Aleph* and *Yod*.
200. *Raysh* is the habitat of the One Energy, its cosmic container.
300. *Sheen* is the mythical "breath," the organic movement of the Universe, *Aleph's* active agent (this is important).
400. *Tav* is the tabernacle—or sanctuary—of *Aleph* in manifestation. Its energy is equal to that of *Aleph*. Without *Tav,* nothing would exist.

In Hebrew, those signs are called *Aut* in the singular and *Autiot* in the plural. We shall be using those words from now on.

Some time ago a rabbi appeared on a television program with a self-appointed cabalist. "God created the world with the *Autiot*," he declared.

Faintly hoping that he had not heard clearly, the host of the program asked, "Do you really mean that God created the world by means of the Hebrew alphabet?"

"Yes, I do," replied the rabbi with no uncertainty.

For emphasis, I want to repeat that those *Autiot* are symbols of different states and aspects of the Cosmic Energy in its living movement. The direction of those movements depends upon the situation. It is either toward *Aleph* or *Taw*. Those two directions coexist in the One energy, which has a dual aspect in order to be aware of itself. The two aspects are "explosion-contraction," or the in-and-out cosmic breathing (an Indian image). There are also other descriptions of these two aspects.

Seven *Autiot* are "doubles." The same letter-number can be pointed or unpointed. The pointed are "hard" and either resist or reflect any inflow of Energy. The unpointed are "soft" and allow the inflow to pass through them. The pronunciation of the letter-number changes slightly to indicate whether it is pointed (see the list below). "The Lord Jesus explained . . . which figures of the letters . . . had points, and which had none."[1]

For readers who are interested in the variations of pronunciations, here is a list that also includes their astrological aspects:

2 $\begin{Bmatrix} \textit{Bayt} \text{ pointed} \\ \textit{Vayt} \text{ unpointed} \end{Bmatrix}$ form Saturn in $\begin{Bmatrix} \text{Aquarius} \\ \text{Capricorn} \end{Bmatrix}$

3 $\begin{Bmatrix} \textit{Ghimel} \text{ pointed} \\ \textit{Djimel} \text{ unpointed} \end{Bmatrix}$ form Jupiter in $\begin{Bmatrix} \text{Sagittarius} \\ \text{Pisces} \end{Bmatrix}$

4 $\begin{Bmatrix} \textit{Dallet} \text{ pointed} \\ \textit{Thallet} \text{ unpointed} \end{Bmatrix}$ form Mars in $\begin{Bmatrix} \text{Aries} \\ \text{Scorpio} \end{Bmatrix}$

20 $\begin{Bmatrix} \textit{Kaf} \text{ pointed} \\ \textit{Khaf} \text{ unpointed} \end{Bmatrix}$ form the Sun—both in Leo

---

[1] *The Lost Books of the Bible*, p. 57.

$$80 \begin{Bmatrix} \textit{Pay} \text{ pointed} \\ \textit{Phay} \text{ unpointed} \end{Bmatrix} \text{ form Venus in } \begin{Bmatrix} \text{Libra} \\ \text{Taurus} \end{Bmatrix}$$

$$200 \begin{Bmatrix} \textit{Raysh} \text{ pointed} \\ \textit{Raysh} \text{ unpointed} \end{Bmatrix} \text{ form Mercury in } \begin{Bmatrix} \text{Gemini} \\ \text{Virgo} \end{Bmatrix}$$

$$400 \begin{Bmatrix} \textit{Tav} \text{ pointed} \\ \textit{Thav} \text{ unpointed} \end{Bmatrix} \text{ form the Moon—both in Cancer}$$

Turning from macrocosm to microcosm, we discover that from *Aleph* to *Tav* the *Autiot* describe in sequence, and with accuracy, the functions of the cell and then the organs. After that, *Raysh-Sheen* emit in opposite directions the flow of organic life, and we see the double spiral of RNA and DNA as a double energy, assimilable or destructive.[2] "The Lord Jesus explained . . . why one letter went before another." Other elements of Cabala show many aspects of the relation between physical and chemical processes.

I have suggested that modern science has to catch up with an ancient science that the Rabbi knew very well. Now I venture to say that we can understand it differently with the added precisions that our rational minds need so we can avoid many past errors. The Second Coming is not to be met with any hysterical, emotional feelings, but with the serious understanding of intelligent adults. So now, with the help of our brief explanations of the letter-numbers, let us get on with the decoding of the word *Satan*, and heal our minds of the fear and disease brought about by that imaginary personage.

---

[2]See my notes on biology functioning with the Hebrew letters (text translated by Jack Hirschman) and a long commentary on the *Sepher Yetsira, In Tree II* (Santa Barbara, CA: Christopher Books, 1971.

Chapter 12

SATAN

SATAN, PRONOUNCED "SAH-TAHN," IS A VERY ancient Hebrew word. It is spelled *Seen-Tayt-Noun* (300-9-700). The first letter is *Seen* or *Sheen*. The symbol for *Seen* differs from *Sheen* only in the way that it is pointed. *Seen* has its point at top-left; *Sheen* has its point at top-right. Both are symbols of the cosmic flow of living energy, call it breath or metabolism or what you will. Both are active agents of *Aleph* in time and space. And, since *Aleph* is infinite, both are necessary agents.

You will never learn from any book or teacher the exact difference between *Seen* and *Sheen*. Understanding that difference belongs to the fulfilling of the Scriptures. Compared to each other, *Seen* can be likened to a laser beam and *Sheen* to diffused light. The action of *Seen* upon any cell is therefore very different from that of *Sheen*. Speaking in general terms, *Sheen* stands for life and vitality in a state of pure being. *Seen* is that same vitality in action, penetrating deeply into the core of everything. The energy of *Sheen* is everywhere present; it operates through the "laser beam" quality of *Seen*. It is *Seen* and not *Sheen* that penetrates our egos, our personal minds, our self-consciousness. Satan's second letter is *Tayt*. *Tayt* symbolizes a cell—any cell. This cell can be a tree, a man, a vegetable, an animal, a tribe, a political cell, et cetera.

The third letter, *Noun* final, stands for the Principle of Indetermination, a very essential factor at stake in the totality of the "cosmic game." This is not the proper place to go into *Noun* in great detail. Let me merely say that it represents an inner freedom of life. Life in its wholeness does not, and cannot, accept circumscription by the proliferation of any "living creature after his kind" (Genesis 1:24)—by an endless repetition of prototypes molded from memories.

Now let's translate that word *Satan* as the Rabbi fired it at Peter. The Rabbi is the *Seen*, the cosmic vitality of living energy penetrating to the very core. Peter is the *Tayt*, the cell. Can the Rabbi get through the cell in order to reach his goal, the final hour? As expressed by the letter *Seen*, the Rabbi is the carrier of a multidimensional energy that coexists and coincides with our four-dimensional, space-time continuum, and that surpasses it in quantity of life and energy. He persistently said that he belongs to those other worlds and that the "Kingdom," as he puts it, is everywhere—but that humans do not perceive it.

In today's vocabulary, this means that our psyches are structured as shells (or cells) enclosing the human consciousness in what we call the "me," the "ego," or the "self." Peter's ego was obviously both strong and immature. The psychological shell named Peter rebukes the Rabbi when he reveals his future sufferings. Peter says, "This shall not be unto thee" (Matthew 16:22). His words express resistance to the flow of life that penetrates into him. By a process of feedback, he exhales that same Energy in its opposite direction. And he does it on his own terms ("those of men, not of God"). He digests the Rabbi's energy and projects it out of his limited mind into an imaginary world of Messiahs, Heavens, and other images.

As far as Peter is concerned, the *Noun* final is not reached by the Rabbi. His infinite energy has not passed through. The Principle of Indetermination, which is the Spirit of Truth, is not attained. We shall develop that theme in more detail in the next chapter. It is very, very important if we are to understand the 2,000 years of institutional churches that follow.

I am not condemning Peter. He was chosen to behave exactly as he did. His reaction to the Rabbi was and still is a necessary and inevitable aspect of the function of the cell, whether physical or psychological. The complementary aspect is, of course, the yielding nonresistance that allows the flow of life to pass through. But if it passes through a sieve, nothing is accomplished.

So here comes Judas, the second "Satan." He operates mysteriously in the darkness of minds, wounding them grievously by introducing into their darkness the light that "shineth in darkness; and the darkness comprehended it not" (John 1:5). (For more detailed information and explanation about Judas, I refer my readers to my preceding books: *The Cipher Of Genesis, The Song Of Songs* and particularly *The Passion of Judas*.[1])

In selecting his twelve disciples, the Rabbi knew exactly what he was doing. And he enacted his whole drama as only the Master of Masters could do it. He chose the two principal characters of his drama according to what they were. Judas understood this. Peter did not.

When Peter later used his self-appointed authority to repeat calumnies against Judas and to arrange the nomination and election of the obscure Matthias as his replacement, he (Peter) was the traitor, not Judas. Judas was victimized because he did what the Rabbi himself could not do. He fulfilled him. But if Peter, like a laser beam projected into starry space, had not acted as he did (and as he is still doing with his church, projecting the Rabbi into the supernatural), that small Rabbi, crucified or not, would have disappeared without leaving any trace of his steps. And if Judas, like a poisoned arrow, had not accepted his role as laser beam, exposing human minds to their own guilt (hence their real hate of him), that small Rabbi, crucified or not, would have disappeared without leaving any trace of his steps. We can now go back to Caesarea-Philippi.

---

[1]Carlo Suarès, *Cipher of Genesis* (York Beach, ME: Samuel Weiser, 1992; *Song of Songs*, trans. George Buchanan (Boston: Shambhala, 1972); and *The Passion of Judas* (Boston: Shambhala, 1973).

Chapter 13

IN CAESAREA

A T THAT TIME, PEOPLE WERE IN SEARCH OF A new god to idolize. The ancient god Pan, who had been brought back to Caesarea, was too old, and no one prayed to him; he was dying. Many people had already replaced him with the young god Jesus, the miraculous rabbi. In their fervor, they wanted to bow down and worship him.

The Rabbi was alarmed at this Hellenistic revival that threatened to take him over and to drag him into a mythology that was totally alien to him. He was not just another deity to adore for a time. He was Israel incarnate, a link between Israel and the universal consciousness, the consciousness of all that is.

But most of the masses around him were seeking a concrete deity to add to their series of gods and goddesses. The rest were Jewish followers with a messianic longing, but their conditioned minds were as hard as rock and cemented to dead traditions. Jews who even today believe in a Messiah to come expect him to be a chief, a king who will reign on earth and lead his people into a "last battle" that will inaugurate the Messianic era of justice and happiness.

The Bible, however, uses the word *Messiah* (or *Anointed*) in a way that is not restricted to a King of Kings. For example, the 45th chapter of Isaiah gives Cyrus the title of "Anointed" (or "Messiah") with these opening words: "thus saith the Lord to his anointed, to Cyrus . . ." The messianic idea had evolved in many different ways by the time the Rabbi arrived. The community referred to in the Dead Sea Scrolls was expecting a Messiah king and a Messiah high priest who would be his hierarchal superior.

The New Testament of the Bible refers to the Rabbi not only as king but also as high priest. In Hebrews (9:11,12) we read: "But Christ being come an high priest of good things to come, by a greater and more perfect tabernacle, not made with hands, that is to say, not of this building; Neither by the blood of goats and calves, but by his own blood he entered in once into the holy place." So this Christ differs from the sacrificial priests of the temple in that he sacrifices his own blood, not the blood of animals. This mystic symbol is more important than we realize: in Hebrew, *Adam*—pronounced Ah-Dahm—means "Aleph in blood." The Rabbi frequently declared himself "Ben-Adam," which means "son of Aleph in blood" but has been mis-translated "son of man" in the New Testament. When the Rabbi "sacrifices" his blood, he liberates the *Aleph*—the timeless energy, his "Father"—from the conditioning and limitations in which it finds itself when "fallen" in blood. By sacrificing his blood, he is not "saving" human beings; he is "saving" the Cosmic Consciousness from its imprisonment in humans. And this true understanding is the opposite of the traditional explanation.

So the Rabbi comes to Caesarea not only to find out what is going on, but chiefly to assert his Hebrewism as opposed to the Hellenistic influence. And much more important, he finds himself in latent conflict with his own disciples.

Actually, the Hebrewism of the Rabbi has more in conflict than in common with the Jewish views of it. The Hebrews became Jews through their Exodus from Egypt. The Exodus was their real birth. They were scarcely concerned with the Creator of the galaxies. Even to this day their God is (out of his innumerable definitions) that one who thus introduced himself to Moses: "I am the Lord thy God, which have brought thee out of the land of Egypt, out of the house of bondage" (Exodus 20:2). This "being brought out of bondage" is the real Genesis of the Jews. They were born at that moment. The Jew is born with his freedom. His God is the explosive power that freed him.

His mission is freedom, a freedom that asserts itself far and wide and obstinately.

In freedom, Abraham talks with God. Jacob fights Him (but is it not God who has attacked Jacob?). Yahweh grants the Jews the right to make mistakes when they insist on having a king to judge them: "And the Lord said unto Samuel, Hearken unto the voice of the people in all that they say unto thee: for they have not rejected thee, but they have rejected me, that I should not reign over them" (I Samuel 8:7). Yahweh grants them the right to exasperate Him to the point that He brings "upon them the king of the Chaldees, who slew their young men . . . and had no compassion . . . and they burnt the house of God . . . and them that had escaped from the sword carried he away to Babylon."

And so it happens that life exacts such wholesale destructions. But more about that later. For the time being, I am still in Caesarea, and I am expecting to be witness to a strange dialogue between two strange characters. First, there is the Rabbi, belonging to worlds so unknown that he left no historical record of his passage. (This reminds me of a charming episode in the *Pistis Sophia*, chapter 12:22: "I entered into the houses of the sphere, shining most exceedingly . . . . and all the rulers and all those who were in that sphere fell into agitation one against another . . . . saying, 'How hath the lord of the universe passed through us without our knowing?'"[1] Isn't that beautifully said? "Passed through us without our knowing.")

So, first there is the Rabbi. And then there is Simon Bar-jo-na, renamed Peter by the Rabbi (Matthew 16:17). He is the "historical" Jew. His mind, his memory, his hopes and dreams are "historical," as are all the Jews in their Jewishness. Cancel history, and no Jews would be left. So the "historical" mind of Simon Bar-jo-na is concentrated upon the battle of the Jews for freedom from the Romans. Has the battle reached the final stage before judgment and victory?

---

[1] G. R. S. Mead, *Pistis Sophia* (London: John M. Watkins, 1955), p. 16.

But the Rabbi is beyond space and time, beyond history, beyond all the succession of events ever recorded by memories. As he has put it, "Before Abraham was, I am" (John 8:58). "And the master . . . said, 'I think that this boy was born before Noah' " (Infancy XX:10, *The Lost Books of the Bible*). What sort of relationship can these two characters have as they face each other at Caesarea? What sort of dialogue?

Chapter 14

THE DIALOGUE OF CONTRADICTION

NOW WE ARE IN CAESAREA WATCHING A drama, an encounter between two archetypes who are opposites in essence. The drama is being staged by the Master of Masters in Cabala: the Rabbi. His contradictory design is to move in the direction he wants, but by means of that which he does not want. In his timeless Cosmic Consciousness he has no grasp of our so-called physical world, and no resources for what we call physical action. If he had, he would be wearing a crown and waving a sword. He would be an ambitious, authoritarian chief waging mortal combat on some immortal battleground. Or, at worst, he would be an unlucky agitator, a premature anarchist, or the Jewish patriot that some exegetists insist he was.

Then there is Simon Bar-jo-na, the personage who became Peter. Nobody I know has ever described him as a mystic. Nobody gives him high marks for intellect. He is solid (the rock), impetuous (the do-gooder who rushes in where fools fear to tread), and positive (but likely to be confused, even to the point of contradiction). When the Rabbi begins to wash the feet of his disciples, Peter blurts out, "Thou shalt never wash my feet" (John 13:8). One verse later he has swung to the other extreme: "Lord, not my feet only, but also my hands and my head."

When Jesus takes Peter, James, and John up into a mountain where he is transfigured before them "and, behold, there appeared unto them Moses and Elias talking with him," Peter cannot remain silent. Impetuously, he suggests building three tabernacles (or tents) for them (Matthew 17:1-4).

When, during the Last Supper, the Rabbi is getting to the point of designating Judas as his messenger, it is Peter who doesn't wait to hear but beckons to John as the obvious choice (John 13:24). It is Peter who, in an uncontrolled moment, draws his sword and cuts off the right ear of the high priest's servant when Jesus is arrested (John 18:10). And when, after the crucifixion, John informs the undiscerning Peter that it is the resurrected Jesus who has been talking to them and giving miraculous fishing instructions to their boat from his position on shore, the naked Peter's immediate reaction is to put on some clothes and then jump into the water (John 21:7).

Peter loves the Rabbi. He would give his life for him. And finally he gives it—but in the wrong direction, as he tends to do (or overdo) almost everything. Peter is crucified head downward—a perfect symbol, whether it actually happened or not. And today, old as he and his church are, Peter is certainly doomed to fulfill this prophecy in John 21:18: "Another shall gird thee, and carry thee whither thou wouldest not."

But back to Caesarea. Peter is waiting and ready for the fight. He is expecting his Messiah to take command of the armies and lead them all to victory and the end of the world. His sword at the ready, Peter is burning to serve the Rabbi, his Messiah—and to serve him better than anybody else. He will be lieutenant, captain, major, colonel, general, chief of staff, the indispensable second in command!

And here is the Rabbi. Who is he? And why has he come to Caesarea? First he questions his disciples: "Whom do men say that I, [Ben-Adam,] am?" (Matthew 16:13). (I have substituted the original "Ben-Adam" for "Son of man" in that quotation. "Son of man" doesn't make sense to me.) The Rabbi sees that the disciples hesitate. They look at each other and don't know exactly what to answer. "And they said, Some say that thou art John the Baptist: some, Elias; and others, Jeremiah, or one of the prophets" (Matthew 16:14). Obviously, they don't know who he is.

The Rabbi insists: "But whom say ye that I am?"

Peter replies, "Thou art the Christ, the Son of the living God."

The Rabbi agrees but then charges his disciples to tell no man that he is Jesus Christ (Matthew 16:14-20). Why? Why must they not proclaim it far and wide as his worshipers have been doing ever since? Some say that he was afraid to have it known. That is absurd, preposterous! So why must the disciples tell no man that he is Jesus Christ? That is the important question!

In Cabala, every person has a true name, a name that is the very person. We are all—each one of us—particular concentrations of energy. And each one of these concentrations can be expressed by one individual combination of letter-numbers. When decoded, that combination gives an exact definition of what the person is in terms of energy.

It is obvious that Jesus is not such a name. We all know that Jesus is not even the Hebrew name of the Rabbi, especially when pronounced "Gee-zuss" in English, "Jay-zew" in French, "Hay-soos" in Spanish, etc. Add to that "Christ" or "Creest" or "Creestow" or 10,000 other pronunciations, and your sounds are merely noises that would not be understood by the disciples.

To know a true name, how to pronounce it, and under what conditions, is a very serious matter. It is to invoke, summon, and call into presence that individual, alive or "dead." It is to make contact. (See I Samuel 28:7-25 for the example of Saul and the woman who calls Samuel from the dead.) Even today the Jews do not allow themselves to pronounce the name YHWH. As I mentioned earlier, very few know how to, and the distortion "Jehovah" is an empty shell.

Jesus' true name includes a *Sheen*, the active agent of *Aleph* in time and space. Earlier we noted that *Sheen* stands for life and vitality in a state of pure being. It is like diffused light that has no power of penetration. John described it when he wrote, "And the light shineth in darkness; and the darkness comprehended it not" (John 1:5). Now the Rabbi needs *Seen*, *Sheen's* very active "twin" that we compared to a laser beam, if he is to penetrate into the psyches (*Tayt*). And he needs two Satan (*Seen-Tayt-Noun*) because of the double function of the psychic cell.

In the dialogue with Peter that we have been discussing, the Rabbi now continues to build the *Tayt* through which he must pass—his *Sheen* having become the *Seen* of Satan. The *Tayt* is this prototype of man that is before him—Peter. And the Rabbi builds Peter up by inflating his "I," his "ego," his personal self. Peter's special calling is this inflation. He has been chosen for that. Must we "die" to our selves, or psyches? Not unless the ego is strong enough to do so. If it does before ripening, it is suicide. If it merely inflates and imagines that such inflation is strength, that, too, is suicide.

So the Rabbi has his two Satan. He will act through Peter's inflated ego and through Judas' cancerous infliction on psyches—the sense of guilt. Later, Paul will never be able to extricate himself from this notion of sin. And thus a powerful, organized religion will be built on a fantastic contradiction—authority and sin. The person called Jesus has indeed not come to bring peace to the minds of his followers.

And now how I wish that I could assume Paul's style by writing, "I exhort you, brothers," or "one more recommendation." I cannot do it because what I have to say is so obvious! In matters of religion, can we stop being theologians, scholars, exegetists? Can we stop being solemn and pompous? Can we do away with the splitting in two of our lives?

One half of our lives is the "every day existence," building and consolidating our minds on the assumption that this world is a solid reality. The "other," as we call it, concerns an imaginary, mythical somewhere in a childish "heaven," a reprint of Mount Olympus on which live the "Holy Family," Father, Mother, Son, and any "Saint" whom we decide to introduce into it. Can we at last see that all the mysteries of all the religions are only screens we have built in order to avoid facing the one fundamental mystery—. consciousness! I went into that subject briefly at the beginning of this book: "How is it that consciousness exists?"

Whatever we are and whoever we are, something is here—something that is irrevocably condemned to be here and to be a mystery to itself.

Let me emphasize again that we are detached fragments of a universal consciousness made of an undetermined number of worlds, having an undetermined number of dimensions, all coexisting and interpenetrating each other. And let me repeat again that in consciousness there are no insulated compartments, no partitions or dividing walls.

The Rabbi is a forerunner of our maturity. He is a consciousness without frontiers. And in Peter, he sees every human being. Just as the Rabbi can pass through what we call walls, so he passes through the shells in which we enclose our minds. And he says of the man Peter who faces him, "I will give unto thee the keys . . . and whatsoever thou shalt bind . . . and . . . loose on earth shall be loosed in heaven" (Matthew 16:19).

What he thus says is true *for every one of us*. Is it not obvious? Where there are no insulated compartments, no partitions or dividing walls, whatever we do has repercussions in the totality of the universes! What a responsibility for every one of us!

And when he is quoted as saying, "thou art Peter and upon this rock I will build my church" (Matthew 16:18), let us reject that translation. The Rabbi did not use the words *Peter, rock, Cephas,* et cetera. He used the Hebrew word *Abben.* Decoded, *Abben* means "Father-Son." In a deeper sense, it is *Aleph* reaching, through us, the final *Noun,* the Principle of Indetermination. In brief, Abben is a successful Satan. And if the Rabbi ever did say to Peter, "I will build my church upon you," he certainly never did say, "You will build your church on me." But that is what Simon-called-Peter did!

Chapter 15

TOO MUCH QUID PRO QUO

WHILE WORKING WITH AN UNCLEAR STATE-ment in Matthew 26:31, I suddenly realized that in quoting the Bible, I may be leading—or, rather, mislead-ing—my readers into the canonical way of thinking. My real intent, of course, is to disentangle their minds from that pitfall. The more we open consciousness to the immeasur-able, the more clearly we see that theologians rewrote the Bible in their own image instead of translating it accurately. What they produced is in general a bizarre barricade against the original revelation. The result tends to be a mess of quid pro quo, blunders manufactured by substituting falsities for truths through ignorance, accident, or design.

According to the passage that I am working with in the King James Version, Jesus says to his disciples, "All ye shall be offended because of me this night." The same passage in the Revised Version reads, "You will all fall away because of me this night." And the French Protestant text by Louis Second reads, "*Je serai pour vous tous, cette nuit, une occasion de chute.*" Three different translations of the same simple quotation! Which, if any, is true?

If we accept "All ye shall be offended because of me this night," we still don't know what Jesus meant. To be offended is to become "resentful of, disgusted with, or angered by." *The Concise Oxford Dictionary* defines *offense* as a "stumbling block, occasion of unbelief." It is not surpris-ing that even today we see Jesus, as Paul put it, "through a glass, darkly" (I Corinthians 13:12). And I am trying to say that the time has come not only to see him clearly "face to face" but to be *in* him.

My constant battle is mostly against the torrents of words that generations of analphabetic theologians have poured over us so that, having ears, we hear garble, and having eyes, we see only shadows. Enough, let us change the subject.

I mentioned earlier the word *sheep*. In Hebrew the plural of that word is *Rehhelim*. Rehhelim is also Rachel (Jacob's beloved) in the masculine plural. That masculine plural can be understood only through the logia of *The Gospel According to Thomas:* "Every woman who makes herself male will enter the Kingdom" (We shall examine the Thomas gospel in a future chapter.)

The Rabbi has a definite link with Rachel and with all that Rachel symbolized. In restricted circles it is known that Jesus as a bodily man was the reincarnation of Jacob (Rachel's husband). Jesus says so in John 13:18, "He that eateth bread with me hath lifted up his heel against me." This statement is a reference to Jacob, whose name is Yaaqov in Hebrew and derived from Aaqav, which means "heel." Jacob and Esau were twins. Esau was born first from Rebekah's womb. "And after that came his brother out, and his hand took hold on Esau's heel; and his name was called Jacob" (Genesis 25:26).

Jesus' statement, "He that eateth bread with me hath lifted up his heel against me," is also a reference to Jacob giving food to Esau when Esau is led to acknowledge that Jacob is the elder. Here Judas is identified as Esau. So the contest of two "enemy brothers"—the "Son" of *Aleph* and the "Son" of *Tav*—ends with the myth of Jesus-Judas.

I have repeated it ad nauseam, but I want you to see how one thing inevitably leads to another in the Bible, both in the Old and New Testaments. No detached fragment makes sense unless we have a total view of the whole. Poor Abel, who is so cruelly murdered by his naughty brother Cain, is not Abel in the original text. He is Hevel. So when the Preacher writes in Ecclesiastes 1:2, "Hevel, all is Hevel," why in the world should it be translated in the King James Version, "Vanity of vanities; all is vanity"?

But let's get back to our two in Caesarea. Peter, over-joyed in his inflated ego because he has "understood" the opposite of what the Rabbi really said, will strive and struggle with all his might and means to reign in this world as Prince of the Apostles. For the time being, his Messiah has gone to heaven. But he will come back. They will resurrect in glory. Heaven awaits us when we are dead.

Peter creates an abyss between Earth and Heaven so as, says he, to establish the Kingdom of Heaven on Earth. He is caught in a maze of contradictions that he will never be able to climb out of.

In Caesarea, he and the Rabbi, *in conuitio oppositorum*, are initiating a fantastic adventure called the Christian Era. Paul will arrive later to launch it.

Chapter 16

AD PERPETUAM REI MEMORIAM

IMPETUOUS, FIERY, AND CONFUSED, PETER HAS decided to take everything upon himself. He is Ab-ben. If the Master fails, Peter will save him in spite of his failure. But if the Master goes to his doom, Peter will be careful not to follow him there. No, not there! When the Rabbi is shackled and sent before the high priest, "Simon Peter stood and warmed himself. They said . . . art not thou also one of his disciples? He denied it, and said, I am not." When asked again, he denied again (John 18:25-27).

Peter is determined to save himself first. After that, he wants to do all that the Master was unable to do. He will take his Master's place. He will establish his own church— but in the name of the Master. He will reign in his name, invent a whole doctrine in his name and declare that the Holy Spirit is upon him. He will be God on earth.

And thus it was that the prodigious energy that was brought forth in him by the Rabbi eventually overflowed in fantastic deeds all over the world—bloody, brutal, cruel, hysterical, violent, sadistic, savage, and . . . sublime. Yes, also sublime in its saints, its arts, its cathedrals, its power-ful personalities, and its incredible explosion today. In this era it is indeed driven by an excess of power. It is being destroyed by an inner explosion caused by that power mis-managed.

Why all this "sound and fury"? Why the mixture of horror and marvels in which nobody distinguishes between error and truth intimately mixed? Why the long-ing for a lost heaven? Why the hypnosis?

Today we are waking up. We are beginning to ask our-selves in all honesty and sincerity if the last twenty centuries ever really existed. The answer is to be found in the condition of consciousness.

I don't believe that the Rabbi on the cross ever had a feeling of being forsaken or abandoned. I don't believe that he uttered his words as quoted in Matthew 27:46: "Jesus cried with a loud voice, saying, Eli, Eli, la-ma sa-bach-tha-ni? that is to say, My God, my God, why hast thou forsaken me?" He never referred to himself as an isolated person with his own temporal mind, and thus susceptible to feeling forsaken or abandoned. If he cried "lama sabachthani" on the cross, he could have been posing the question only to us, not to God!

Actually, the Hebrew root *Sabakah* means a lattice, a trellis, a net. I am therefore inclined to think that, completely lucid and at the point of leaving this limited body, he wondered aloud how his infinite consciousness had been caught and contained in the net of a human, limited form, and reduced in proportion.

This concept of infinite mind contained in a human body is difficult for many moderns to understand. I imagine that it was just as incomprehensible at that time. But it appears again in *The Gospel According to Thomas* (L. 28-29). There he marvels at how the spirit, "that great wealth," has made its home "in the poverty of flesh."

This is a very important point, perhaps more than all others. The Rabbi's consciousness, fully alive and freed on the cross, is astonished at having been caught in the net, the maze, the labyrinth of that dying body's consciousness. To my mind, that is how we must examine the 2,000 years that have elapsed since then. I suggest that you try looking at your daily existence as seen, so to speak, from a great height. In other words, get out of your human being and look at it nailed to its daily cross. And as you see that self pinned to its daily existence of repetitive motions, consider your true individuality as consciousness that has no insulated compartments or dividing walls. Then you, too, may begin to ask what you are doing in such a shell, in such a mess.

So that, to me, is the question the Rabbi shouted from the cross. He shouted it to us, and we have not heard it. His worshipers are falsely led to believe that he came to save their petty human minds and that they, as personal entities, are being saved by his death. I positively say and insist that the opposite is true. He came to save the Cosmic Consciousness from what we call "us!" I say that his question on the cross is: "*Why?* Why are we so?" It is a devastating question when we begin to understand it.

This calls for a somewhat lengthy explanation. When we study objectively the belief of salvation, we discover that it is a sequel to a very old Jewish superstition. Let me suggest we never forget that the Rabbi was a traditional Jew. So were almost all of his disciples. Thus it is not surprising to discover that many Jewish traditions found their way into what became the Christian church, despite the fact that the church fathers did what they could to detach their branch of the cult from the original trunk.

According to the old rabbinical beliefs, death entered the world through sin—either through Adam's "original sin" (a concept that came from an erroneous reading about "forbidden fruit" in the Bible) or through one's personal sins. Although the Talmud (Shabbath, 55b) gives a list of persons alleged to have died without having sinned, tradition agrees with the pessimistic view in Ecclesiastes 7:20: "For there is not a just man upon earth, that doeth good, and sinneth not." The syllogism is simple: all sinners are mortal; all men are sinners; ergo, all men are mortal.

It is true that in biblical times there was a vague notion that something survives after death—or, rather, that human beings have been given an immortal something called "breath." As we read in Genesis 2:7, "And the Lord God formed man of the dust of the ground, and breathed into his nostrils the breath of life; and man became a living soul." If man is a "living soul," why all this dramatic sinning, dying, being redeemed, and resurrecting? And, for that matter, why did this "redeemer" called Jesus have to come? I rather think that he came to remind us that we real-

ly are projections of living souls—if we know how to give
birth to living souls and how to allow them to grow and
take fire!

But following Paul's nightmare about sin, the
Christian religion has tended to adopt the old rabbinical
notion that at some uncertain future date the bodies of the
dead will rise from their graves. According to the Jewish
religion, it is sacrilegious to remove tombs because the
dead have supposedly gone vertically down in the earth
into a region called Sheol and would not find the way back
to their bodies if the tombs were taken away. When, for
instance, Samuel is called from the dead in the biblical
episode we mentioned earlier, he comes from under the
ground.

If Moses and Elias appear on a mountain with the
Rabbi, it is because they enjoy a special status: they have
not died! True, the case for Moses is a bit dubious, but he
did disappear without anyone finding his body. The situation with Elias (or Elijah) is more clear-cut: everybody
knows that he was carried "up" in a chariot of fire. And is
he not the precursor of the Messiah? "Behold, I will send
you Elijah the prophet before the coming of the great and
dreadful day of the Lord" (Malachi 4:5).

In conclusion, I think it would be useful to understand
the beliefs and superstitions of the Jews whom the Rabbi
was teaching and thereby discover the origin of the notion
of salvation. If we don't, we risk falling into a theology
without the proper foundation. Most valuable is the realization that many Christians have unknowingly adopted
an Hebraic psychological structure while imagining that
nothing is further from the fact. As for the Jews, they fail to
understand that the Rabbi's real message is the very
essence of Israel. In rejecting that message, they have with-
drawn from their inner revelation while imagining that
they are still in it. As another Ecclesiastes with a clearer
view, I would proclaim, "Contradiction of contradictions:
all is contradiction."

For the Rabbi, it was of primary importance that the
memory of his Coming should remain. The energy that he

injected into our space-time continuum could not and cannot ever disappear. It can be compared to an exalted kind of radiation that will never be dispelled. Still it was important that the coming of this energy be linked forever to his appearance. And he knew that such memories would not live on unless they also included the violent, brutal, intolerant reactions of psyches enraged by the denial of their apparently solid world. It was not surprising for psyches to deny that which denied their reality. Nor was it surprising for such psyches to attempt to punish, kill, and forever destroy the Rabbi by crucifixion. The contradiction had to be given a start. The Rabbi knew it. He would be remembered by its opposite: the Church.

Ad perpetuam rei memoriam. Did the Holy See know perhaps what it was doing?

Chapter 17

TO DIE FROM NOT DYING

THE RABBI UNDERSTOOD CLEARLY THAT THE "original sin" of the human mind is its animal origin. His own thought was infinitely expanded by the penetration of spheres of consciousness outside of our dimensions. These spheres of consciousness penetrate into our dimensions and are present here, but our limited human minds remain closed to them. The Rabbi wanted to open and liberate our thought from its purely sensory, materialistic character. The average, so-called normal human mind frequently feels that it has sinned or is sinful. Since the sin or guilt is the human mind itself, how can it escape?

What a strange, crazy experience! That mysterious phenomenon called consciousness, that Mystery of mysteries in which there are no insulated compartments, no partitions or dividing walls, is imprisoned in a space-time universe and can't find its way out. Consciousness knows in its innermost being that it is eternal and immortal. So thought reasons, "If I die, it must be because I am guilty, I am a sinner." But the mind that says that is the mortal mind of the body. And it is precisely that mind that must die, just as the body dies.

The Rabbi took care of that problem before anything else. He said in effect that you are not the body that you consider guilty and that your true consciousness is not sinful. He told us not to identify ourselves with our bodies and not to say that our "father in flesh" is our father. He suggested that we say, as he said, that "my Father" (the origin of my consciousness) is "in Heaven" (in the cosmos). I come from it, and I return to it. He who sees me in my present condition sees the Father (infinite consciousness), and it is the same for every one of you if you become as I am.

Through that opening gushed a tremendous flow of energy. But that energy (or what was left of it) was confiscated by the most materialistic minds and all the sluggishness that they could pile up: institutions, doctrines, rituals, idolatry, confessions, inquisitions, holy wars, and repetitions and repetitions and repetitions of prayers for sinners.

The Rabbi knew it would happen that way—that his teaching would fall upon general misunderstanding because the time for a psychic mutation had not yet come. His words were quickly twisted into inverted hints of truth and so became hollow footprints in the sands of history. Still, the threshold of mutation was already evident. Since the One Life is double in its existence and manifestation, the Rabbi had to act doubly: physically by introducing it into the linear time that we call history, and psychologically by a mysterious action in the womb of the era that was to come.

To initiate this double action, the Rabbi chose Caesarea where he would be standing in opposition to the god Caesar. This was the beginning. Next, he introduced Satan into Peter by building up Peter's personal ego through a marvelous misunderstanding. Then came his dramatic announcement of his forthcoming death that would not be the death of his consciousness because it belongs to another dimension. He promises to come back afterward and make himself known in order to prove that we do not die and therefore are not sinners. And he clearly states that he is one with us. Therefore, our nature is not different than his.

Peter understood that when he wrote, "For Christ also hath once suffered for sins . . . that he might bring us to God, being put to death in the flesh, but quickened by the Spirit" (I Peter 3:18). Peter never believed in the resurrection of the physical body. "Christ once suffered," he wrote. Once, and only once, because the death of the body is an inevitable suffering.

As for the Rabbi's being "quickened (or made alive) by the Spirit," Peter has once again gone off the track and back to Satan. Immersed in the temporal, his "down-to-earth" mind invents a fantasy about bodily life in some wonderful place called Heaven that turns out to be almost a carbon copy of Mount Olympus. According to Peter, that "quickening," or resurrection, becomes for us something far off in the future that we may find after death when our soul is taken back by God. (Did we borrow it from Him?) And heaven is considered to be a perfect place far up in space. At that time the earth was not known as a globe in a galaxy but as a disk with a celestial cupola above. Mortals trod the earth, and the Olympian gods were above on top of the cupola, each one having his own specialty much as the saints now do.

Gradually such "Christian" propaganda addressed to the growing masses built up that picture and encouraged more and more idolatry. When this revival of mythology needed a Goddess, the "Virgin Mary" was cast for the role. Statues of her became idols to be prayed to and worshiped. That was the end of the Revelation, and the beginning of Peter's Church.

So for the next 2,000 years the most sincere minds search with all their might for the life of Spirit but exhaust their vitality in futile, fruitless battles against the flesh. Foundering in the Paulist contradictions, and just as unable as Paul to free themselves from the notion of sin, they persistently "see through a glass darkly." They get lost in a labyrinth of mirrors with no exit. At each turn they vainly anticipate salvation and revelation but are faced only with their own disappointed image.

Disciplines, fastings, privations. Readings, prayers, rituals. Repetitions and repetitions and repetitions. Always the same. Always the struggle for personal salvation. Always the not-dying to oneself. And all of this finally numbs or assassinates, so that now and then a certain fictitious "peace be still" is fabricated that quiets the fearful and faithless. Alas! this is what it is to die from not-dying.

Chapter 18

ARE WE STILLBORN?

HOW AND WHY DID THE RABBI AT CAESAREA encourage misunderstanding in Simon, son of Jona? Jona, pronounced "Yonah" in Hebrew, is a dove. The dove has always been the symbol of Israel. By emphasizing that word at that time in that place, the Rabbi gave Simon the flattering notion that he had materialized from the dove of the Holy Spirit. Was the Rabbi inflating the disciple's ego in order to build his Satan? In the very next sentence he added to the inflation by giving Simon the new name Peter, or "rock."

Actually, the Rabbi was not deceived. He knew what Peter was and what he would be, just as he understood Judas, whom he seemed to leave in the shadows while really preparing him for his important role. In emphasizing the name Jona, the Rabbi actually cast an extraordinary light on the deathly opposition between Peter and the Jews— and also on the contrast between Peter's Church and the Rabbi. This is not easy to understand unless one is trained to think along a double contradictory circuit.

Until the very last moment Peter did not believe that the Rabbi would be crucified. Such a death upset all of his hopes and dreams. His love for his Master changed his Messianic views. For him, the Rabbi became a metaphysical being who had taken physical shape for awhile. Thus Peter "had seen the next-to-God of Israel." This interpretation did not seem to him anything strange or out of tradition.

Such projections of the deity are to be found all through the Bible. For instance, the story is told in Exodus 24:9-11, "Then went up Moses, and Aaron, Nadab, and

Abihu, and seventy of the elders of Israel: and they saw the God of Israel: and there was under his feet as it were a paved work of a sapphire stone, and as it were the body of heaven in his clearness. And upon the nobles of the children of Israel he laid not his hand: also they saw God, and did eat and drink."

Surely this means that they were not dreaming. The God had actually materialized. But here enters the inevitable law of contradiction that the Bible knows so well and that the Rabbi masters splendidly. The minds of the people cannot help materializing everything. I have said that many times, and I hope that you will excuse me if I continue to repeat it over and over again. The last quotation from Exodus illustrates it vividly: Moses and the others have seen God so clearly that they can describe Him (or It) in detail.

What can the Rabbi do to inject into hard, conditioned minds an Energy that must shatter them in order to penetrate into them? Please, think it out! Can he simply "take these minds by the hand," so to speak, and lead them in their current condition into his multidimensional worlds? If you travel as a suitcase full of junk, you will reach your destination as a suitcase full of junk. You cannot rely upon something that you imagine and name the Holy Spirit to alter you during the journey.

The Rabbi came at a time when masses of human beings had been driven into slavery and were badly in need of human status. It was a time when the Jews refused to submit to Rome and fought until death or deportation destroyed their lives and homes. As the active agent of YHWH, the Rabbi found himself in the same situation as YHWH described in Exodus 3:9-10: "Now therefore, behold, the cry of the children of Israel is come unto me: and I have also seen the oppression wherewith the Egyptians oppress them. Come now therefore, and I will send thee [Moses] unto Pharaoh, that thou mayest bring forth my people the children of Israel out of Egypt."

A little later YHWH adds, "Now shalt thou see what I will do to Pharaoh: for with a strong hand shall he let them go, and with a strong hand shall he drive them out of his land (Exodus 6:1). And in order to be clearly understood, YHWH explains how He will do it: "I have hardened his heart, and the heart of his servants. . . ." (Exodus 10:1). So "the Lord hardened Pharaoh's heart, and he would not let the children of Israel go" (Exodus 10:20).

Perhaps you imagine that this is an unusual, paradoxical procedure. It is not. It obeys the absolute law of the one universal Energy in its eternal birth through the action of its apparent inner contradiction. It is the perpetual motor— or mover—of history (Karl Marx saw a bit of it). It is the inner drive of the human consciousness in its development toward maturity. If you know how to read the Bible, you will see this from beginning to end. You will also see how psyches react ferociously against the apparent contradiction, like wounded animals ready to maim and kill. And you may also learn that there is something better to do than to beg Jesus to help you out of your trouble. When you are *in* him, there is no need for help. Instead, there is a part to play in the "cruel" life on earth. The Rabbi obeyed the Law. He gave his followers enough to be persecuted and to persecute—enough to be perpetually in a state of unrest and conflict. Exodus was a birth. The Rabbi now presents a much greater birth that has spread all over the world.

Were the Jews persecuted by Pharaoh? So were the early Christians by Rome. This is not unusual. Joshua destroyed entire populations and devastated their lands in order to establish his kingdom—all with the blessing of YHWH. So did Peter, as soon as he had the chance. And by Peter, I mean his Church. It grew in power, established its domination over nations and populations, and took dictatorial authority over everything from birth to death and beyond. It terrorized, tortured, imprisoned, executed, doomed or blessed, excommunicated or anaesthetized, and demanded, in a word, *submission!* But something more than earthly power was at stake: the maturity of the human being. It was always made to appear as a future promise: a promised land promised by a hypothetical YHWH, and a promised salvation promised by Peter—a "salvation ready to be revealed in the last time" (whatever that means) and a "hope to the end for the grace that is to be brought unto you at the revelation of Jesus Christ" (I Peter 1:5,13).

For Peter, the Revelation is yet to come. But the Rabbi had explained how to achieve *now* that maturity others offered only as a possible future gift. He said, "Whosoever will come after me [will follow me in the integrity of his own being], let him deny himself [his limited earthly consciousness], and take up his cross [the so-called matter on which he is nailed], and follow me" (Mark 8:34).

In Hebrew, the word for "cross" is *Tselev*. According to the code, it is the constructing factor that builds a container. In this case, the container is our limited self. To "take up the cross" means to gather up all the elements constituting our ego, or self—all that builds the prison walls of our captive awareness—and to present it at the threshold of mutation, total change. *Tav*, 400, the last letter in the Hebrew alphabet, was a cross in the ancient graphics.

The Rabbi said, "Except a man be born again, he cannot see the kingdom of God" (John 3:3). Then he emphasized, "Ye must be born again" (John 3:7). But who gets born, and who gives birth? How do we deliver ourselves without a miscarriage?

That which is true physically (the physical world is only a projection) is also true psychologically. It is true historically (history is the illusion of the running on and on of linear time). And it is true in the deepest realms of Cosmic Consciousness. The process of the One Life is One.

And now, to end this chapter, here I am again in Caesarea-Philippi as a witness to an apparently crazy dialogue. I am there, not in imagination nor in a time long past. I am there now, being one of whom Jesus said, "If I will that he tarry till I come, what is that to thee? follow thou me" (John 21:22). If I have waited all this time (this time that is of no time and in which there is no waiting) so as to give testimony of the timeless Jacob and of the life of Israel and of the presence of the Rabbi and of the deeds of Peter as initiators of the universality of humankind, what is that to you?

And if I wish to say, "Thus saith the Lord, Israel is my son, even my firstborn" (Exodus 4:22) to all Pharaohs big or small, temporal or spiritual, heads of States or heads of Churches (all in hierarchical order and authority—white, black, yellow, or otherwise-colored skins), what is it to them? It is up to all to know if they are alive or stillborn.

Chapter 19

OR CAN WE LIVE A DEATH?

NO PEOPLE ON EARTH DO LIVE OR EVER HAVE lived the sublime and tragic game of Cosmic Contradictions as have the Jews. No other people have so projected into human consciousness the passion of that perpetual life-death, which murders us in a resurrection that fulfills us. Simon-Peter-Pope-Pharaoh, instrument of oppression that is today obsolete, has accomplished his mission. The human is now born to its cosmic vocation. The ripening is there. This is the Second Coming of the Rabbi!

It has always been taught that the conditioned ego is despicable, that one must put an end to it in order to find the cosmic self again. And it has been taught that we must die to our personal selves by means of all kinds of virtuous practices and sacrifices and exercises, the first of these being total obedience to authority. Still others teach that we must grow our brotherhood to the point of worldwide unity, or all become a collective unit of some kind, or stop thinking altogether and, like a drop of water, lose the self and become one in the ocean of Life.

Formulas are not lacking. They come in packages marked "physical" and "metaphysical," "political" and "religious," et cetera. They come from the West, and they come from the East—from Rome, Jerusalem, Mecca, Benares, Tokyo, Peking, Moscow, and Washington, D.C. And didn't this book begin by calling for this "death to one's self?" "If the seed dies not . . ." Yes, we know all that. But what if the seed dies before ripening? And what if the fruit dries on the trees? Teaching and preaching that the shell of consciousness (the "I am") be destroyed before it is fully matured is advocating suicide. The ego must develop until it is strong enough to break its own shell through an inner, natural process of development.

Ever since Israel first declared itself to itself and to the world, Hebrews have lived the dramatic event of the genesis of cosmic man, and they have narrated it. Joseph, son of Jacob, directs his people to settle in the Egyptian womb. They develop in a favorable environment until their growth inside the womb brings on the first contractions and birth pains. Then Pharaoh oppresses them. When the time for delivery comes, YHWH intensifies Pharaoh's opposition to achieve the expulsion of the newborn.

Is that a contradictory action? Not at all. It is a double action. From that moment on, the Jews become the temporal shell of "intemporality." They try to project this "intemporality" into the temporal, and that produces a really contradictory situation!

Moshay (Moses) is the mythical character who triggers the movement. Both his name and his story identify him as "Fire in Water." As with Moses, so with the Rabbi: their symbolic similarities appear everywhere. For example, there is this common penetration of the cosmic "Fire" into "Water," the primal element. Moses is "Fire in Water." Later, John the Baptist baptizes with "water," and Jesus with the "fire" of Spirit.

At YHWH's command Moses goes up the mountain of Nebo to be shown the promised land in the distance—and to die, "but no man knoweth of his sepulchre unto this day" (Joshua 34:6). The body of Moses disappears. So does the body of Jesus.

And the Rabbi brings liberation from slavery, just as Moses liberated his people from bondage. Here again is contradiction playing its game. The Jews free themselves from slavery only to put themselves into self-made chains. They chain themselves down with so many laws that they become law. Codes, statutes, ordinances, regulations, precepts, rules, decrees, commandments! Every hour of the day, every day of the week, and every week of the year they build their monolith: the rabbinical law.

And Paul, the most rabbinical of apostles, struggles hopelessly to disentangle himself from the Law that he wants to replace with Faith. His struggle inspires in him his most dramatic and obscure utterances: "For I was alive without the law once: but when the commandment came, sin revived, and I died. And the commandment, which was ordained to life, I found to be unto death. For sin, taking occasion by the commandment, deceived me, and by it slew me. Wherefore the law is holy, and the commandment holy, and just, and good" (Romans 7:9-12).

No doubt the Jews chained themselves to Law because of the explosive nature of Cosmic Energy. They built themselves into steel-plated safes in order to contain the explosive germ they carried in their flesh. But they did not want to know—as they do not want to know today—that historically they are persistently faithful to themselves in acting against themselves as "containers" to be shattered at every moment by the explosive Energy they "contain."

At particularly significant times, the released Energy becomes tremendous. It is always a terrible ordeal for the Jews. Their suffering is beyond description; and the human consciousness attains new dimensions.

Caught as he was in the intense vibration between "containers" and "contained," Paul could only be in a state of confusion, and propagate that confusion. Peter tried to build his Church as a powerful "container." We shall get back to him in a future chapter. Right now I think we should take a quick flight over the centuries.

First we see God seated on his platform, as he appeared to the ancient Jews. Then we see Moses coming down from his mountaintop, carrying his celebrated Ten Commandments, including "Thou shalt not kill" (Exodus 20:13). When he spies the Golden Calf, he goes into a rage. "And he said unto them, Thus saith the Lord God of Israel, Put every man his sword by his side, and go in and out from gate to gate throughout the camp, and slay every man his brother, and every man his companion, and every man his neighbour" (Exodus 32:27).

Three thousand men were killed that day. "Thou shalt not kill?" No wonder Moses broke his faked tablets after that incident!

So we go on traveling and read that "the Lord had said unto Moses, Say unto the children of Israel, Ye are a stiff-necked people: I will come into the midst of thee in a moment and consume thee: therefore now put off thy ornaments from thee, that I may know what to do unto thee" (Exodus 33:5). Having seen Him with a sapphire stone under his feet (Exodus 24:10), can they go to Him and beg forgiveness for their ornaments? No, sir! So YHWH hits them again: "And he said, Thou canst not see my face: for there shall no man see me, and live" (Exodus 33:20).

He constantly overwhelms his people with cursed blessings and blessed curses. He promises a land of milk and honey, but that land must be conquered through wholesale genocides. Why not? He helps Joshua in that massacre, even to the extent of stopping the sun in its well-known circuit around the disc called earth.

So on to the next stop on our itinerary. Joshua is a preview of what Peter will be. He establishes his temporal power. But the Jews are such strong "containers" of YHWH that they resist him successfully for many centuries.

Let's hurry on to the period when the Jews have elected Judges to judge them. Gradually we see the corruption setting in and the day when both Judges and people are so perverted that they deny YHWH. "Then all the elders of Israel . . . . said unto him [Samuel] . . . . now make us a king to judge us like all the nations. But the thing displeased Samuel . . . . and Samuel prayed unto the Lord. And the Lord said unto Samuel, Hearken unto the voice of the people in all that they say unto thee: for they have not rejected thee, but they have rejected me that I should reign over them" (I Samuel 8:4-7).

Here the Jews have displayed their "right to err." It is a most important and decisive step when one stands up and declares, "I have the right to make mistakes." Samuel clearly sees that when the temporal and eternal (the two contrasting flows of power coexisting in the One Energy) are at grips, they react to each other for and against. But when the temporal, compressive power rejects the flow of timeless-ness (the eternal) in favor of a temporal kingdom, it cuts the flow of energy and assumes its right to go to its death and destruction. (I presume this fact to be the ontological origin of the superstition that man is mortal because he is a sinner. It refers to "another" death and "another" error.)

To resume our flight over historical events: we see the Jewish kingdom being very quickly disrupted. (Who ever attributed wisdom to Solomon?) We see two miserable kingdoms full of murders, conspiracies, idolatries, wars, and disasters. For how many centuries? Seven, maybe, since Moses. And finally Jerusalem is too corrupt, too dis-eased, and too out of joint to be repaired. Then YHWH intervenes again—drastically this time.

> Therefore he brought upon them the king of the Chaldees, who slew their young men with the sword in the house of their sanctuary, and had no compassion upon young man or maiden, old man, or him that stooped for age: he gave them all into his hand. And all the vessels of the house of God, great and small, and the treasures of the house of the Lord, and the treasures of the king, and of his princes; all these he brought to Babylon. And they burnt the house of God, and brake down the wall of Jerusalem, and burnt all the palaces thereof with fire, and destroyed all the goodly vessels thereof. And them that had escaped from the sword car-ried he away to Babylon; where they were ser-vants to him and his sons until the reign of the kingdom of Persia: To fulfil the word of the Lord by the mouth of Jeremiah, until the land had enjoyed her sabbaths: for as long as she lay deso-late she kept sabbath, to fulfil threescore and ten years (II Chronicles 36:17-21).

Let's stop a moment to meditate on the sublimity of this incident—and then hurry on. After the Chronicles of this devastation comes the book of Ezra. A few Jews return to Jerusalem from captivity. They have forgotten everything, even their language. Everything is new. This is still another birth. Ezra recommences all that Moses had done. And here is even the conqueror of these conquered, King Cyrus of Persia, now acknowledging YHWH and promoting the reconstruction of the temple at Jerusalem. And here I stop reading because there is really nothing more in the book except for the marriage of Esther.

It is a symbolic episode during a period that is half asleep and barely disturbed by the echo of voices coming from Isaiah, Jeremiah, Ezekiel, Daniel, and other minor prophets. It is a sort of approximate *modus vivendi*.

But the ferment of revolt never rests. We come to the battles with the Asiatic kings and condense them all into one symbolic name: Maccabees. The forty years of Maccabean revolts—a parallel to the forty years in the desert during the Exodus—are forerunners of that which is coming: Rome.

And here she rises: Rome, the tolerator of all religions as long as they include her gods. Rome, installing a Jupiter in YHWH's temple. We now witness the most fantastic of all combats—one against a thousand, the fight without hope on the material plane. And here again is a symbol, Massadah! On this rock men, women, and children discover the impossibility of ever losing their identities—of no longer being themselves. They discover that they have been able only to "kill each other to the last man." This discovery marks a decisive step on the road to true individuality without return. All that precedes this discovery is only prenatal. Don't call it "the human condition."

Chapter 20

THE NINTH OF THE MONTH OF AV

A ND NOW I SEE IN ONE PICTURE THE DESTRUC-
tion of the temple by Titus, the dispersion of the Jews,
the last and lost battles, the final tragedy, and the coming of
the Rabbi, with another tragic end. I see all this as one single event. It is a tremendous psychological happening, a
projection on our space-time screen of a blinding, piercing
ray—a bolt of lightning from the very heart and soul and
being of Israel, which lives in multidimensional spheres.

The cosmic life brought by the Rabbi was born on
Earth. It shattered its shell—the Jews. Its message reached
the hearts of the suffering people. But the representatives
of Jewish law were not able to accept it as the expression of
what they had been fighting and dying for during all those
centuries. Israel, they reasoned, would bring peace ad justice to this world. Israel would unite the people and create
a perfect fraternity. But what does this rabbi mean by pro-
claiming, "Israel is my first born, says YHWH," and then
adding, "I am that first born, that Israel"?

Even more important, Israel must have a clear, inner
knowledge of the universal energy. But that very ancient
science that was given in custody to Abraham has not been
revealed by the Rabbi. Only its "perfume," so to speak, has
been manifested.

In a mighty resurgence of vitality, the Jewish tree then
grew some of its most beautiful branches. With reverence,
I shall here name only Reb Aqivah, the father of the Talmud
and Cabala, and Simeon Bar Yohai, whose light is still not
extinct today. (Speaking generally—and remember that
this is only a bird's-eye view)—the synagogue ignored the
Jewish revival of the Cabala. The revival became dormant,

and the Cabala remained secret for a millennium plus a few centuries. Then mystics unknown to the Mediterranean people found it and began to work with what others called "strange thoughts and habits." This chapter of Jewish history is fascinating and important, but it is not our subject for today.)

Now that the Second Coming is here, I want to point out some aspects of it as they relate to the First Coming. I hope to open the door to further investigations (after the world's so-called religious passions, prejudices, and emotions die down) on the "extravagant and quaint" lack of relationship between the Church, the Rabbi, the Christians, and the Jews. The destruction of the temple occurred on "the 9th of the month of Av." Later, several disasters fell upon the Jews. All of them took place on the 9th of the month of Av! As a result, that date has become a day of mourning for traditional Jews.

According to the Cabala, the names of the Hebrew months are symbolic. Each of them expresses a different state and process of Energy. The Cabala teaches that YHWH with the letter *Tayt* (the cell) forms the month of Av. And *Tayt* is 9. "The 9 of the month of Av!"

Av is *Aleph* (the supreme, living, infinite energy) plus *Vayt* (its container). And what is "the Tayt of Av?" No exact translation is possible, but it can be roughly defined as "the cell that starts the organism of a father-in-flesh." Without any possible doubt, the 9th of Av is the day of renewal, the birth of a "new past" that follows the death of the "old past."

As "the cell," *Tayt* is so well known in some Asiatic countries that the coming of spring is celebrated with "festivities of Tayt." *Tayt* is renewal, new life budding. The Rabbi said, "Ye must be born again" (John 3:7). And again and again.

What a contrast to the day of mourning celebrated by traditional Jews! Why are Jews weeping and lamenting the fall of obsolete structures instead of rejoicing in the freshness of the new that is coming into being? And where is the newness that was brought 2,000 years ago? "We must be new," Paul exclaims, but he does not achieve that newness.

Instead, he is stubbornly "determined" to know only Christ crucified (I Corinthians 2:2). Is that a "new" image—that image of a dead God, hanging in misery on his instrument of torture? Where is his resurrection?

Millions of multitudes sing and dance and eat and drink joyfully together when spring comes. But does any one of the participants take that single step forward to true *individuation*? It seems to me that they all stay where they are or retreat in the opposite direction. They become "new" only in the sense that the plant is new that in its flowering repeats and repeats its same old prototypes. There is nothing "new" there in the absolute sense of the word. The truly "new" is produced only by a total, simultaneous destruction or end of the "old."

Our vegetable and animal renewals are all repetitions of the old prototypes with everything "after their kind"—grass, herb, tree, fruit, fish, fowl, cattle, beast, and serpent (Genesis 1: 11,12,21,24,25). But read carefully on and you will find no mention of "after their kind" repetitions for man—"man in his own image, in the image of God" (Genesis 1:26-31). This iteration and reiteration of "after their kind" repetitions does not hold true for the human psychological cell. I have tried to demonstrate this in our examinations of the word *Satan*. I have tried to show the total breakthrough there.

The flow of energy brought by the Rabbi produced strange results. Identified with the compressive function of the human psychological cell, Peter became the oppressor Pharaoh. Judas, the explosive energy introduced into psyche, was rejected by the psyche in self-defense. The Jews rejected Peter, who did everything he could to be rejected by them. And the name Judas became synonymous with traitor and Jew in the misled minds of Christians.

But with the Second Coming, Peter as Pharaoh is obviously done for. Judas, as Jesus' twin brother, is the one to resurrect.[1] And the Rabbi does not require resurrection. He has, of course, always been here.

---

[1]See Carlo Suarès, *The Passion of Judas* (Boston: Shambhala, 1973).

Chapter 21

JEWS AND GOD UPROOTED

TWO THOUSAND YEARS OR SO AGO THE JEWS gave birth to YHWH. In other words, the divine Immanence that abides permanently in the Jews exploded. It is not a Titus who destroyed the temple. It is YHWH, bursting out of its shell and exploding as a collective dream into a supposed incarnation named Jesus Christ.

Experts cannot find any mention of Jesus in historical records. Historians in general agree that the Jesus of the Gospels never existed. This should not surprise us. As we have pointed out before, all that is produced in the linear time called history and in the limited space called geography is only a projection of our dreams of events that are happening in many other dimensions. Besides, does it really matter whether a person named Jesus actually existed?

The Eternal appeared so clearly that it needed only a timeless instant to strike like lightning. The important point is that Israel has struck! It is an explosive grenade whose fragments are hurled in every possible direction.

I can imagine that the energy that shot through our limited universe required fifteen outlets: the Rabbi as fulcrum, John the Baptist, the twelve apostles, and Paul. The twelve were told repeatedly by the Rabbi that they had been chosen. With Paul, they scattered all over the world— from Ethiopia to Scandinavia, from Spain to India— spreading everywhere the power that issued from the Jews.

Does that mean that contradiction came to an end? Certainly not. Contradiction intensified, multiplied, and became unbelievably atrocious. The power that issued from the Jews was turned against the Jews. It was now aimed at destroying them. For 2,000 years that no longer exist the world smashes, suppresses, tortures, kills, and exterminates Jews. It is an effort to destroy Israel physically and morally so that this "thing" will not upset the world again, so that YHWH will not return. The God Jesus has been comfortably packed away in some place called Heaven. But by the process I call *contradiction*, this excommunication is the very thing that will make him return. And this is what I call the Second Coming of the Rabbi.

The Jews lost their earthly center. Uprooted, they continued to live for only one reason: they could not die. Destroy all the holy shrines—Jerusalem, Mecca, Benares, temples, churches, cathedrals—and the human species generally becomes as bewildered as babes torn from their mothers. In that condition, they will follow anybody anywhere. Oddly, this did not happen to the Jews. They were not permitted to be led astray in perplexity and confusion—to follow anybody anywhere. Their persecutors saw to that. No Jew was allowed to forget his Jewishness. Far from it. In the end, the persecutions of the Jews actually recreated, rebuilt, and restructured the Jewish psyche.

The Rabbi brought immense hope to the small community around Jerusalem. The repression by their Roman conquerors had been cruel. Rome did not accept rebels, and these rebels would not accept Rome. The Romans could not obtain submission. They managed to occupy the territory only by continued strength of arms. As always happens in such cases, the occupiers finally found a local, institutional power that was willing to cooperate with them. This power was the synagogue, which had always been in conflict with its saints and prophets (the common condition of organized churches). The fathers of this new "Christian" Church made a colossal mistake by creating a religion based upon a God who is subject to death. It doesn't make sense.

I have often spoken to members of Christian churches (particularly the Roman Catholic Church) about Cosmic Consciousness that is infinitely, eternally alive and creative.

Their most frequent response is, "I'm not interested. My God is Jesus." Yes, Jesus has become God to them. And I declare that a God Jesus dead on his cross is a false god. By what metaphysical or ontological necessity has this church, which is a lateral branch of the Hebrew tree, so persistently tried to detach itself from the original trunk? Is it condemning itself to wither and die from lack of roots and fresh sap?

Chapter 22

PETER

W E ARE BACK IN CAESAREA. LET'S TAKE ANOTHER
look at Peter. I want to show you the technique he
used so that he would be cast off by the Jews. Forgive me if
I repeat a few details.

"Whom do men say that I am?" the Rabbi asks his disciples.

They give several vague answers.

"But whom say ye that I am?" he demands.

"Thou art the Christ," replies Simon Barjona, suddenly become the Hebrew equivalent of Peter. Immediately he
is struck with an intense, immense radiation from the
Rabbi. It is like a body blow to his entire being. He will
never recover from it.

Is the Rabbi something different from what Peter had
imagined? Is he something else entirely? The disciple
begins to wonder. For the first time, he is uncertain. Maybe
he is even sorry for some of the things he has promised. In
confusion, he contradicts the Rabbi's foretelling of his coming crucifixion and resurrection, and receives a second
body blow: "Get thee behind me, Satan: thou art an offence
to me" (Matthew 16:23).

Finally Peter misunderstands the Rabbi completely,
and forever after imagines that the Rabbi has come only for
a short time in order to announce that he will be coming
permanently some other time in the near future. And that
misunderstanding dictates to Peter what he believes to be
his duty: he must spread the word about the Rabbi's coming return and keep everybody in a proper state of expectation during the waiting period. Peter will consecrate his
life to that, and he will succeed. To him, the end of the

world is near. It will come before the passing of another generation. Peter will carry his cross. If necessary, he will lose his life, knowing full well that he will retrieve it soon again when the Rabbi descends gloriously from Heaven on a cloud. So Peter goes to work with Paul, and they gather as many people as they can and prepare them for that great, miraculous day. Paul preaches to the uncircumcised, and Peter takes care of the circumcised. In so doing, Peter puts into action the craziest quid pro quo ever known on earth.

Perhaps you recall my comments on these words alleged to have been said by the Rabbi to Peter: "Whatsoever thou shalt bind on earth shall be bound in heaven: and whatsoever thou shalt loose on earth shall be loosed in heaven" (Matthew 16:19). I observed that, since consciousness is without boundaries, whatever anyone does in this world to set minds free is done in every sphere. Obviously the aim is for all of us to do whatever we can to create an awakened and enlightened state of freedom. Unfortunately Peter took it to mean that he alone was the one to have the capacity of "binding and loosing." And he also believed that his duty was to *bind*! He was determined to fasten and attach together all the souls he could, and to hold them together by the exercise of authority and every other possible means. They must be bound and carried into Heaven lest the Devil bind them and carry them into Hell. (We have all seen iconographs of the Devil chaining souls and driving them into the fire.)

The germ of Inquisition was thus sown in Caesarea-Philippi. It was in that state of mind that Peter approached the Jews. The New Testament of the Bible includes two of his Epistles. They are sufficient to show us his method. And they illustrate the deliberate manner he has adopted that exasperated the Jews to the point of creating an insuperable gulf between him and them.

The necessity of contemporary humans is to free our minds and thus discover universal consciousness. We can no longer avoid taking a critical look at an institution that for so many centuries has given itself the fundamental task of "binding" instead of "loosing," constraining spirits instead of freeing them, and thus blocking the penetration of the universal into each one individually. It is in this spirit that we now examine the Epistles, particularly those of Peter. No doubt they have been altered and tampered with by apostolic successors. So by "Peter," we can include and understand the ensemble of these men and their work. Let it be added that many, many adherents of this Church have not read these Bible texts for one reason or another—either because they are not interested or because they are obedient to authorities who teach them that their missal, or mass book, will suffice.

So here [with the author's comments in brackets] are a few significant passages from the First Epistle General of Peter—and they sound as though they were addressed to the Jews with the objective of keeping them out of the Church:

"Peter, an apostle of Jesus Christ, to the strangers scattered throughout Pontus, Galatia, Cappadocia, Asia, and Bithnyia" (1:1) [in other words, to the dispersed Jews];

"Elect . . . unto obedience" (1:2) [this, don't forget, is addressed to rebellious, unsubmissive Jews who for centuries have been unmanageable even by "God Almighty"];

"and sprinkling of the blood of Jesus Christ" (1:2) [haven't the Jews seen their own blood shed everywhere?];

"Blessed be the God and Father of our Lord Jesus Christ" (1:3) [hasn't YHWH declared himself the Father of *all* Israel?];

"which according to his abundant mercy hath begotten us again unto a lively hope" (1:3) [hope is rooted in the Jews even when lamenting their disasters];

". . . To an inheritance . . . reserved in heaven for you" (1:4) [this is the reverse of the self-appointed mission of the Jews—the establishment of justice on Earth];

". . . ready to be revealed in the last time" (1:5) [For Jews, this is a fundamental error. Peter says that the Revelation will come at the end of the world. What for? To Jews, the Revelation has been here since Abraham.];

"Wherein ye greatly rejoice" (1:6) [Rejoice? These people in such great grief, sorrow, desolation, devastation?];

". . . though now for a season, if need be, ye are in heaviness through manifold temptations" (1:6) [It's been a "season" of many centuries! And what temptations?];

"Wherefore gird up the loins of your mind, be sober" (1:13) [Sober? We are chased out of the ruins of everything we once had. We are killed, tortured, crucified, and our wounds are still open. We have run out of tears for our dead. "Be sober?" Give us some water to drink before we die of thirst.];

"As obedient children" (1:14) [Children? We Jews who are among the oldest people on earth? We who have traversed all human history? We who have battled for thirteen centuries against the world and ourselves because we carry in our blood the stupendous knowledge of the One Life in its contradictory power? We who have grappled with life— its joys, its madness, its horror, its splendor? And who are we to be obedient? The Spirit obeys only the Necessity of the Father. And obedience to that Necessity is Freedom];

". . . Submit yourselves to every ordinance of man . . . whether it be to the king, as supreme; or unto governors . . ." (2:13-14) [No comment necessary];

". . . Servants, be subject to your masters with all fear; not only to the good and gentle, but also to the froward" (2:18) [No comment];

"Likewise, ye wives, be in subjection to your own husbands" [No comment];

"Likewise, ye husbands, dwell with them . . . as unto the weaker vessel" (3:7) [No comment];

"Feed the flock of God . . . being ensamples to the flock" [*Baaa!*];

"Likewise, ye younger, submit yourselves unto the elder" (5:5) [No comment];

"Humble yourselves therefore under the mighty hand of God" (5:6) [Here is the Pope pontiff. The hand of God, with Peter as trustee?];

"Be sober, be vigilant; because your adversary the devil, as a roaring lion, walketh about, seeking whom he may devour" (5:8) [Aw, go to hell!].

Chapter 23

IMPERIALISM

PETER, A JEW, COULD NOT IGNORE THE VERY foundation of the Jewish mind—rebellion against any organization built upon injustice. For Jews the Messianic concept, no matter how illusory it might be in its different manifestations, inevitably includes the establishment of justice on Earth. A dream? Perhaps. But Peter tried to impose upon them faith in a Revelation and justice that awaited them in some future heaven at some uncertain time. To Jews this was a deceptive promise that promised nothing.

Since Peter could not get the Jews to change, he turned in the opposite direction and founded his enterprise on the defeat of Jewry and of Hebrew practices. Peter inaugurated a technique that is still being used today. He cemented the foundation of his Church with anti-Semitism. It solidified. The anti-Semitism fabricated by the Church formed the Church and was prominent in the development of a religious empire. Peter needed this issue. Until he got it, he had been promising nothing but mythical hopes and dreams because he had nothing else to offer. He didn't know then and doesn't know now that the Revelation has taken place and that there is nothing more that needs to happen except our opening ourselves to it.

That revelation has come again today, not through metaphysical acrobatics and prayers, but through our new scientific approach, which is discovering the all-embracing fact that Cosmic Energy is Life, that all Life is Consciousness, and that all Consciousness is within us and without any limitations. We have only to open ourselves to it. And to open ourselves to it, we need only one thing: we need to be *new*!

Paul tried to present this newness that is so obvious today, and failed. He was to hazy about it, and he admitted it. He had met the Rabbi only once, and then as an apparition— ".a light from heaven" (Acts 9:3), a bolt of lightning that left him blind for three days. Paul's entire apostleship had a supernatural character. He felt the impact of other worlds that he must enter, but he saw "through a glass, darkly." He was like a caterpillar in his chrysalis who knew that he was a butterfly but could not yet get out and fly. Beware of such states! They are deceptive. The "waiting to be reborn" can be a creator of false images based upon one's old beliefs and new imaginations. In truth, the "wanting to become" is stagnation. The "being now" is Life.

It is in "waiting to become" that Paul touches us. But Paul is not yet ripe, and the times are not yet ripe. In his prenatal condition, Paul feels his fertilization. It had been produced in that lightning illumination on the road to Damascus, and that illumination is himself. He could not let it pass without "fixing" it in consciousness. But to "fix" it is to restrain it or stop it. What a contradiction!

So Paul propagated a stagnation that became mere mythology. The result was a repressive organization that spread throughout the world the most spectacular whirl of contradictions ever recorded in human history. The fabulous power introduced by the Rabbi was perverted in every possible way. It triggered a series of explosions that during the next 2,000 years (which is really only two days) made human beings take 2,000 giant steps forward for the one step they had managed until then.

After all this must come the final true acceleration in which everything explodes. The structure in which eternal consciousness has been locked must be shattered. This that is born has broken through its shell.

All of history will be retold in terms of the development of this germ of true consciousness, and no longer in the fictitious measurements of our calendars. Centuries never have the same duration. "In that time" might better be called "in the time of that speed, or activity, or under-standing." The time of today may be something else entire-ly since it has a different "speed" and meaning. Thus the fabulous power introduced by the Rabbi may have started only two days ago since "one day is with the Lord as a thousand years, and a thousand years as one day" (II Peter 3:8). I would say that it is starting now. Time as a spiral in accelerated motion is meeting its axis. Its itinerary as past, present, and future no longer exists.

The ancient historical times are but a dream. I remem-ber that dream. "In that time" the Roman gods were at death's door. Some Greek gods had been disinterred and brought back to prop up the divinity assumed by the God Caesar. The empire was crumbling under the weight of the barbarians. And there was outcry against the subversive Jews!

What is Israel doing in the midst of all that confusion? The destruction of Jerusalem had projected a celestial star on the land of Nazareth. The fire that had been lit by that illumination would not go out. The martyrs thrown to the wild beasts exhaled it as they died. Rome was destroyed because she had destroyed. And since it was her time to die, she had found the way to do so. The new could have started and grown from that ending. But everything went on much as it had before. The empire only changed its vest-ment. The Rabbi, who had never been a god, was named God because of the deeply anchored, mythical necessity that says the killer of a god becomes a god in his turn.

Contradiction! This new Caesar lived in an inaccessi-ble heaven. He was not accessible because he was only the mythological embodiment of a truth that belongs to multi-dimensional universes that transcend ours (he becomes transcendental, "beyond the bounds of human thought") but that penetrates ours (he becomes immanent, indwelling, and subjective).

Contradiction! The transcendency and immanency of this "God of peace" set the stage for the human comedy of religious wars and persecutions on which the curtain falls today. But those battles built Peter's throne! Peter reigned by crushing the evangelical immanence with an authoritarian transcendency. And this authoritarian transcendency became identified only with himself and his Church. But the cosmic energy always works: this compressive force finally provoked the explosions named Luther and Calvin and, today, us.

Chapter 24

MYSTERIUM ECCLESIA?

"OH MY GOD, I FIRMLY BELIEVE YOU ARE ONE God in three divine Persons, Father, Son and Holy Spirit. I believe that your divine son became man, died for our sins, and that he will come to judge the living and the dead. I believe these and all the truths which the Holy Catholic Church teaches because You have revealed them, who can neither deceive nor be deceived. Amen."

I wonder how many of those who utter this Act of Faith understand what they are saying. Those words fall far short of including all of the patriarchs, prophets, evangelists, and others who have presented the Revelation. This is usurpation, not only by Peter but also by an apostolic body that builds a Church and a "truth" in its own image. Doctrine is created or changed according to the disposition of church authorities. It can be carried out by threats and punishments. From Peter to Paul to the village priest, fear is the powerful weapon.

Peter set the pattern when he wrote, "The Lord knoweth how to deliver the godly out of temptations, and to reserve the unjust unto the day of judgment to be punished: But chiefly them that walk after the flesh in the lust of uncleanness, and despise government" (II Peter 9:10). Paul echoed it in Romans 13:1: "Let every soul be subject unto the higher powers." These citations are selected at random. Many more of a similar nature can be found with just a casual reading of the New Testament.

Today "the crisis of the Church" has become a popular subject of conversation almost everywhere. Actually what is occurring is not a crisis but a "double death." The first death is that of the archaic thinking from which churches and synagogues have suffered for centuries. The second is the death of authority, which inevitably leads to the destruction of Rome.

Some reformed churches are beginning to rejoice in the announcement of the Return of the Rabbi. Already I am having friendly, even brotherly contacts with members of those churches. Those who reject me are usually stubborn old-timers who wave the Bible over their heads like a battle-ax and roar, "This is the Word of God!"

From the synagogues, I hear nothing. Theirs is a silent contempt with only an occasional muttering, "What is a Jew who steps outside the Laws of Moses and our traditions?"

It is all very logical. The current "crisis" or disease concerns our understanding of "the Word of God." This Word was originally experienced and described by men who today are mostly anonymous. They transmitted it orally. In many cases the Word was later written down inaccurately by those who had not experienced the Revelation. Translated into many languages, it was rewritten with still more errors. And the rewriting had to be tempered in order to gain the approval of temporal authorities who had little or no understanding. It is not surprising that after centuries of such battering, this rock of revelation should crumble into sand that blows in our eyes and hinders our vision.

But now we are beyond this. We are in the jump of Jacob beyond time. We are in the power of the Rabbi, in the fulfillment of the inner core of the Scriptures. And this inner treasure that has been so incoherently disguised and covered up, suddenly appears to be incredibly intelligible and intelligent. It resurrects in glory and splendor.

The original code of the letter-numbers that I have given is the only instrument that saves and reveals the message of the Old and New Testaments. The Bible is now free from the childishness of old canonical interpretations. A simple goodwill and newness of mind is sufficient to liberate us from all of the old beliefs and inner resistances. This code of the sacred language frees us from linear time and projects us into a timeless eternity. But how many of us will be needed and how much energy and patience and perseverance and single-mindedness will be required in order to break down the anti-truth fortresses that have been strengthened day after day for 2,000 and 5,000 years! And how can we all come to see that these dramatic conflicts are simply the result of our refusal to be born to the cosmic consciousness?

In the last few years we have had an invasion of so-called new translations of the Bible. Unfortunately all of them ignore the original code. The result is a kind of competition in flatness and dullness and variations that are even more erroneous than the old, consecrated texts.

We read and reread that "in the beginning God created the heaven and the earth" (Genesis 1:1). It is a dreamlike explanation of how it is that anything exists, but does not explain how it is that God exists. And the Earth, this "flat disk" that is the only place where life exists, becomes the only job of this deity sitting on top of his celestial cupola and coming down at times in human shape to walk in his Garden of Eden. He is a forgetful God who, after having created everything else in a jiffy, has to go into a delicate operation to extract a woman from a man. In the long run, the operation turns out badly, and the other stories are just as absurd.

A lady asked me the other day, "What does it matter if people believe these stories? After all, what harm does it do?" What harm? Read what it inspired Paul to write later in I Timothy 2:12-15: "But I suffer not a woman to teach, nor to usurp authority over the man, but to be in silence. For Adam was first formed, then Eve. And Adam was not deceived, but the woman being deceived was in the transgression. Notwithstanding she shall be saved in childbearing, if they continue in faith and charity and holiness with sobriety."

What harm? Do you want more quotations? They are not hard to find because everything goes along that ridiculous line. For instance, I Corinthians 11:8 and its following verses: "For the man is not of the woman; but the woman of the man. Neither was the man created for the woman;

but the woman for the man." Et cetera. That's not enough? Then learn, woman, your domestic duties according to Ephesians 5:22,23: "Wives, submit yourselves unto your husbands. . . . for the husband is the head of the wife, even as Christ is the head of the church," and so on and on and on.

When will these Bible texts be considered seriously? When will we decide that the Bible must be rethought from beginning to end? When will we do something about it? There is a drastic revolution to come. It will be brought on by our New Era.

Peter and Paul contributed to the mutilation of the feminine half of humanity, the half that is most closely in contact with the realities of life. The result was that the male half, which tends to live in dreams of conquest and glory, rode the dreams, galloped off on crusades, charged into holy and unholy wars, killed and killed and killed, and carried the torch of the Inquisition.

The archetype of a womanhood that is forbidden enjoyment of the body became a Mother who remained a Virgin. What a logical conclusion! And what a useful model! That Mother, forever weeping over the corpse of her resurrected Son, is the Church's goad that spurs us on to shed emotional tears, beat our breasts in contrition, call ourselves hopeless sinners (although made in the image and likeness of God!), and submit to the total authority of the Church in the hope of absolution.

The pixilated man who took a hammer to Michelangelo's statue of that weeping woman and dead God was perhaps inaugurating our New Era in his own fashion!

As it goes on today, the reading of the Bible tends to putrefy consciousness. It corrupts minds with dead archaisms. It blocks the road to truth and leads only to fairy tales, confusion, and impossibilities. On the other hand, the reading of the Bible in its original code is an integral part of the Second Coming. It releases the long-lost essence and goes far beyond what we can even try to imagine. This dramatic revision is an urgent task for churches now threatened by this Return of the Rabbi. I am astonished that this revision has not yet begun.

I am even more astonished that some important representatives of reformed churches are looking to the Vatican to work out what they call a "common strategy" in regard to the Gospels. Oddly, they see in the Papal authority "a solid bulwark for the essential truth of the Gospels," as if Truth needs bulwarks. Certainly bulwarks are the specialty of Rome, but they are bulwarks erected for the purposes of Rome alone. And those bulwarks are the very cause of Rome's decay.

Rome answered the appeal for united action with a militant operation: it published *Mysterium Ecclesia*, which reaffirms its own infallibility. Obviously, any agreement or accord must call for the subjection if not surrender of her so-called partners.

Chapter 25

IS THIS THE APOCALYPSE?

IT SEEMS TO ME THAT NOW IS THE TIME TO STOP A moment and summarize some elementary points that I have been trying to make. There is a consciousness that goes far beyond our space-time continuum. This consciousness is always immanent, inherent, innate, indwelling. "[T]he kingdom of God is within you" (Luke 17:21). But this consciousness only intermittently opens up a conscious passage through our psyches. It has been seen and felt at certain periods in our limited time sense—a sense that exists only in human thinking as it is concerned with our daily, circumscribed activities.

One of those times of Cosmic Consciousness occurred during the governorship of Pontius Pilate in Judea. The supertemporal awareness was made manifest at a place between Galilee and Jerusalem. That appearance is "past history" only in the dream of limited, space-time minds that remain subject to their own so-called physical projections. (We have learned from physicists that solid objects are actually whirls of energy as "empty" as space.) In other words, the event is not historical in the sense of past, present, and future. The event is psychological. It is historical only for minds that are half awake and half dreaming.

Now please consider the following very carefully and seriously: in "non-time" the event is always here, always present. "The Kingdom of the Father is spread upon the earth and men do not see it" (*Gospel of Thomas*, logia 113). In other words, the Cosmic Consciousness is here even if we say that it is not perceived by limited "space-time" minds. And it is definitely felt intermittently as dramatic shocks produced inside the dream.

The dream state does not know what hits it: it is aware only of the feeling. (From inside your room, you don't see and thus do not know that it is the "big bad wolf" who is hammering down your door; you only hear the noise.) So the psyche almost always reacts to the irruption by resisting this "break-in" and by trying to protect its unreal structures. In other words, the psyches do not "go with" their Cosmic Consciousness that has given the shock. Instead, they tend to run in the opposite direction and to fight for their unreal and unsatisfactory lives with all their blind might and desperate cruelty. Thus they create such liturgies as the destruction of Jerusalem, the cruel dispersion of the Jews, and their wholesale murder by psyches enraged with fear and hate and misunderstanding.

To put it briefly and bluntly, there is a total attachment to earthly values while supposedly worshiping heavenly values. The crux (or cross) of the matter is the impossibility of following the Rabbi's teaching in any organized society. What responsible government would long survive with a policy of love for the enemies of the nation, of taking no thought for tomorrow?

If Cosmic Consciousness is a purely individual matter, then why are we enmeshed in Christian organizations and all the rest of it? Honest Christians today know they are not living the Gospel. Instead, they have succumbed to a convenient morality that goes hand in hand with competition, conflict, conceit, deceit, vanity, ostentation, and so on.

Only a few sects have laws and regulations for a healthier way of life and try sincerely to follow them. Generally they turn out to be variations of Judaism. Like traditional Jews, they inevitably get stuck inside a rigid mold of set patterns. Their thoughts are dictated to them, which means that consciousness becomes filled with concepts and dreams of an imagined celestial world. And the images in this dream are most effective in prolonging their sleep at the very moment when we are all called upon to wake up.

In dream duration we have had 2,000 years of cruel nightmares, in which every thought generates its own contradictions. For instance, the revolt of the Spirit against gods fabricated by temporal powers came to subdue such powers. But the triumphant Church that was born from this revolt resorted to oppression, and thus provoked more upheavals and revolts in an uninterrupted chain.

The perpetual presence of an "absent God" became the perpetual presence of the Devil. The hunt for witches became the royal road to divinity. And somehow Satan, Evil, Demon, Belial always took the shape of "the other man," my opponent in religion, politics, business, love, or anything else. Thus the world has fallen into conflicts without solution or end. It seems to have lost its balance forever. Contradiction of contradictions, everything has become contradiction!

But in such a hopeless state, the fact is that the Church has finally lost its power to oppress. It can try to lead the United Nations, the Red Cross or the Boy Scouts, but nobody follows. It can preach "Peace, Peace," but it cannot even conceive of such a peace, much less install it. Nothing matters now. The Church is torn from the inside. and it is inside that she explodes.

In like manner, the Jewish State will be torn from the inside and must explode. Thus must end the myth of a God who promises her a world—promises her this land of Canaan that was damned by Noah. Thus must end all states, kingdoms, organizations, and institutions. All sovereignties and supreme authorities must explode, for that is the outer effect of the Second Coming.

Is this the Apocalypse? Is this "the end of time"? Is the passing of time so swift today because it is racing to its end? "And the angel . . . sware by him that liveth for ever and ever . . . that there should be time no longer" (Revelation 11:5,6). Every millenium brings the fear or hope of "the end of the world." The World will not end: our world will.

In any case, I do not understand why so many people are so frightened about the fate of humanity. We all know that within a century or a little longer, no current inhabitant of this planet will still be here. We all will have gone. But gone where? Will we be in that well-known jeweler's paradise described in Revelation as a city of pure gold whose foundations are garnished with all manner of precious stones—jasper, sapphire, chalcedony, emerald, sardonyx, sardius, chrysolyte, beryl, topaz, chrysoprasus, jacinth, and amethyst! And the twelve gates are twelve pearls, and the street is of pure gold.

". . . The kings of the earth do bring their glory and honour into it" (Revelation 21:24). And that great, luxurious heaven, which seems to be reserved in exclusive fashion for a chosen clientele, offers a breathtaking spectacle of angels, trumpets, thrones (one with a river flowing out of it), trees that bear fruit every month, and no nights so that there is no need to bring candles or the sun.

And now I am out of breath! This delirious account has been a best-seller for century after century. Almost everybody has read it, but nobody has ever understood it. Perhaps it is so effective precisely because it is incomprehensible. Every day psyches realize that they cannot penetrate the mystery of being born, living, and dying. They want explanations, and faked explanations are given to them. But in their deepest regions of thought and feeling, they know that no explanation solves the problem. So there grows in them a deep necessity to be reminded that mystery (particularly the mystery of death) remains. Not being able to solve the mystery, the psyche plunges into all sorts of images, liturgies, and theatrical displays that distract it from common daily problems. But the displays must be beautiful, and *not* understandable. The day-to-day mind no longer wants to understand. It claims its right to be ignorant. It has this need not to understand. It is enough if it can feel that this daily world is not all there is.

The chief attractions of Catholic cathedrals are their mysterious environments and the masses that are usually delivered in an unknown language. People feel that they are in the antechamber of "other worlds." Thus the new fashion of well-lighted churches and liturgy in the vernacular is a frustration to naive multitudes. They get the impression that somebody is closing the doors to Heaven.

So it is well that the Bible still finishes with this incomprehensible grand finale called The Revelation of St. John the Divine. The curtain comes down on a multitude of contradictory images crashing into each other and casting a magic spell. It is a hypnotic phantasmagoria of labyrinthine mysteries that certainly does not end like any ordinary mystery novel—with a clear, proper solution.

Chapter 26

THE CARDINAL POINT

IF WE HAD ONLY MARK AND LUKE TO RELY UPON, we would not find much in the Gospels to support what I have been saying. Matthew gives some glimpses of it, but only John throws full light on the subject.

Among the canonical writers, John is the one who clearly sees the cardinal point of human consciousness. (Later we shall go into *The Gospel According to Thomas*, which is not in the Bible but helps us to understand other dimensions belonging to other universes.) Undoubtedly John knew and said more than appears in his written Gospel. Perhaps he had forgotten some of the Rabbi's words by the time he decided late in life to write his book. Since then, translations, interpolations, and the changes of word meanings from century to century have obviously made the message hazier still. Today it is almost necessary to have the spiritual understanding already alive within us before we can find it in John. At any rate, let us now work with the gospels such as we have them today.

After many other prophets, patriarchs, and judges (real or imaginary but nonetheless wondrous), a miraculous rabbi arrived to teach the Jews. What were his miracles? Let us set aside his healings of diseases and expulsions of devils, which psychiatrists and psychologists frequently call something else. And the dead whom he brought back to life? There is room for skepticism here since enthusiastic disciples, in a crazy overbidding, attributed dozens if not hundreds of such revivals to themselves.

What about the multiplication of the bread, the walking on water, and other such wonders? Nothing unusual. One can witness them every day in India. And the parables? They were told much earlier in history as Jewish folk-lore. His torture and crucifixion? History is made up of millions of tortured and murdered people. And his reappearances after his death? The dead appear regularly in haunted houses. They deliver messages at séances and walk the earth in new bodies.

There is nothing really unique or important in such incidents. What is unique and important in the Rabbi is far beyond such stories. John saw what it was. He told it as best he could. And this is the axis or cardinal point around which everything turns.

John's account of the Rabbi's prayer at the Last Supper includes words that are the summit of everything that has ever been said. They are well known, but are they understood? Without a doubt they come from what I call multi-dimensional worlds. In this prayer, the bodily son of a new edition of Jupiter disappears. So do the religions that unperceiving others built upon him. The God who creates a terrestrial disk and sits on a celestial cupola in the sky no longer exists. He has been put on the shelf with idols and archaic divinities who have so inefficiently tried to take care of human affairs for so long.

Today the material space universe with its linear time of days and years has lost its absolute reality. Aided by scientific research, we have discovered an indeterminate number of universes in an indeterminate number of dimensions. Now we can see all of these universes as one single living and conscious unity. We can understand this consciousness as everywhere, even if we are not everywhere conscious of its being.

Just as our consciousness-of-being-an-individual is made up of consciousness-not-conscious-of-being (such as our body cells), so we can conceive of a universal consciousness that results from the consciousness of all elements, including that which exists in the gravity of electromagnetic energy up to worlds of infinite dimensions.

Having gone to certain limits of scientific research, we still find ourselves in that mystery of mysteries—consciousness. When we try to discover what conscious consciousness is made of, we discover thought. When we try to discover what thought is made of, we discover language. And when we try to discover what our words are made of, we discover that they contain only images relating to our space-time continuum.

But now consciousness refuses to confine itself to a space-time universe of limits and limitations. It sees that it has manufactured this limited conditioning, but it also sees that it is more—much more—than this limited universe. The modern scientific mind sees clearly that the creation of the world as we imagine it from the ordinary reading of the Bible is erroneous. Limited, erroneous thinking has projected a limited, erroneous self. And we now understand that this self is not the real self.

In sum, we have reached the situation spoken of by Paul in I Corinthians 13:12: "For now we see through a glass, darkly; but then face to face: now I know in part; but then shall I know even as also I am known." And the problem is to reach II Corinthians 3:18: "But we all, with open face beholding as in a glass the glory of the Lord, are changed into the same image from glory to glory, even as by the Spirit of the Lord." This is the glass seen from the other side. And seen from the other side, the seeing has no duration. It is timeless, eternal.

To think as "no time" is impossible. Thinking requires time to think. So we must renounce thinking if we are not to go on indefinitely with such time-bound contradictory thoughts as, "In the beginning" (but there is neither beginning nor ending in the timeless), "God" (who is this God?), "created" (but there is no past), et cetera. And all this the Rabbi knew. And now it is up to us to uncover and discover the true meaning of his words that have been covered by mythology.

Perhaps there is no better place to start than with John 17:5: "And now, O Father, glorify thou me with thine own self with the glory which I had with thee before the world was." These words are uttered by a fully individualized soul that is aware of being and of having been "with" and "as" the Cosmic Consciousness even before it ever projected itself into space-time creations. It has accomplished its Hebraic cycle and will return to itself as it is—cosmic. The text continues, "I have manifested thy name unto the men which thou gavest me out of the world: thine they were, and thou gavest them me; and they have kept thy word."

Have I repeated often enough that in consciousness there are no insulated compartments, no partitions or dividing walls? But whatever one writes can be misunderstood. Please remember that I have never said that every one of the billions of cells in my body knows what I am talking about. Still every cell is alive. Every cell shares my bloodstream and has some sort of consciousness. If we talk to plants and love them, they respond. That does not mean that plants understand your words any more than you understand all foreign languages.

Regarding the words of the Rabbi just quoted from John 17:6, let us be aware that we can be "in him." Then what he says becomes an obvious statement. But if we have manacled our minds to a more limited sense of being, we shall either reject his words as erroneous and without true meaning, or else we shall accept them merely as theological dogma or metaphysical dream stuff.

It is our job to find out where we really stand. In saying the Biblical words quoted above, the Rabbi indicates that he has transcended his human status as a Jew and rabbi. The words come from beyond our particular manifested world. They are heard by a few men with whom he has an "out of this world" relationship. In my terminology, their multidimensional souls are linked in a kind of network or circulation system through which flows universal, conscious Life.

At times my remarks about Peter, Paul, and others sound sarcastic and perhaps critical. I do not mean to suggest that they have not "kept the Father's word." The Word was simply distorted, as it could not help but be. The "Spirit of Truth," as it was then called, had to wait for further development of knowledge in order to be seen in its true, scientific sense. A number of us are now calling to each other in many different voices in our efforts to reestablish an adequate passage of higher awareness through all psyches.

The following words from John 17:20-26 may help. They make up the prayer that I would call the Rabbi's testament or covenant. They are exalted and wonderful!

> Neither pray I for these alone, but for them also which shall believe on me through their word; That they all may be one; as thou, Father, art in me, and I in thee, that they also may be one in us: that the world may believe that thou hast sent me.

> And the glory which thou gavest me I have given them: that they may be one, even as we are one: I in them, and thou in me, that they may be made perfect in one; and that the world may know that thou hast sent me, and hast loved them, as thou hast loved me.

> Father, I will that they also, whom thou hast given me, be with me where I am; that they may behold my glory, which thou hast given me: for thou lovedst me before the foundation of the world.

> O righteous Father, the world hath not known thee: but I have known thee, and these have known that thou hast sent me.

> And I have declared unto them thy name, and will declare it: that the love wherewith thou hast loved me may be in them, and I in them.

Chapter 27

DON'T GET EMOTIONAL!

MORE THAN ANYTHING ELSE THAT I HAVE EVER read or heard, the sublime words of the Rabbi (John 17:20-26) best express the Oneness and Wholeness that we see but do not necessarily attain simply by reading them. Unfortunately some readers probably fell into an emotional haze at the end of the last chapter. Don't get emotional! We must keep common sense and self-criticism alive. Emotionalism simply stops where it is and considers anything further to be anticlimactic.

Anticlimactic indeed! Let's get on.

In this "theological prayer," which I prefer to call his testament, the Rabbi has let the Cosmic Energy—alive and conscious—come forth as best he could. He has transmitted it to those to whom "he has been sent." This was his task, and he has "achieved his work." They in their turn shall have the task of transmitting it to others, either well or badly (and it turns out to be more badly than well).

It is *Aleph* that speaks through the Rabbi—the eternal *Aleph* that is eternally alive but cannot live as temporal. It is very important to understand this: *Aleph* cannot put itself into flesh, but it has "power over all flesh." by the *Lammed* (30) in its name, this A.L.Ph transforms inorganic energy into organic life. Brought to maturity, organic life returns to itself as that state of consciousness in which there are no insulated compartments, no partitions, or dividing walls.

To be One in Unity is not at all this emotional search for an ever-loving, ever-peaceful collectivity that is the fashionable crusade today. When we are *in* him, all errors fall away. These include all translations of the Bible as it is currently read, all doctrines and creeds and liturgies created for the declared purpose of worshiping him, and all organized churches. Everything must fall away because *in* him we are in the foundation of our world and all worlds. We are inside the Mystery of Consciousness. We are in the eternal, timeless Present. We are cognizant of "everything," meaning all of the errors that have been leading humankind until now.

For the moment we can and do quote words that the Rabbi said or that others interpret him as having said 2,000 years ago. But in quoting them, we understand that those words are irrelevant. Then what is so particular or unique about his Coming, if it ever did occur? This is an event that history did not record. Still it is an event so important that it started an era on which we base even our calendar!

And what about the swamis, gurus, and other self-qualified experts come to convert the West to the East? Why should we go to the East when we are already faced with our own gigantic riddle to unravel: the absurdities of the Bible, intimately linked to its holiness. When fulfilled, that contradiction (contradictions again!) teaches us more than any Asiatic wisdom. It is life itself lived and perverted. We must learn to respect the innermost hidden core of the Bible. This means that we must discard every mere word of it, because every word perverts!

I have repeated that over and over again. Every word that tries to convey energies coming from worlds beyond our dimensions is always and inevitably interpreted in terms of our space-time continuum. The "obviousness" of our world (similar to the obviousness of our dreamworld when we are asleep) prevails, so we accept centuries of crazy projections and mythologies as realities.

Even more than exhorting you to beware of Asiatic so-called wisdom (have they done any better than we in their social structures?), I most strongly advise you to beware of all preachers of "Jesus Christ!" They misinterpret and repeat obsolete words in the most archaic ways of thinking. They gather crowds of thousands and hundreds of thousands; and the larger the crowd, the more ignorant is the approach.

It is frequently said that meeting "Jesus Christ" is an easy, simple, sentimental, and emotional (if not hysterical) experience. Beware of such easy ways. Nobody says that it is easy to become a genius, and what we are discussing here is far beyond most of our so-called geniuses. Even our best genius is generally somebody whose awareness and cosmic penetration are far from being *in* the universal consciousness!

And now I hear personal questions bombarding me from all directions. Who are you to declare yourself *in* him? Are you claiming to be even more than a genius? An apostle come back to earth? A gnostic initiate? Of course, I say nothing of that sort. There are already too many people exclaiming, "I am this" or "I am that." The higher they place themselves in the human or celestial hierarchy, the further we should get away from them. What I can say and do say is that I know who I am. And perhaps you will receive the answer by reading this extract from logia 3 of *The Gospel of Thomas*: "If you (will) know yourselves, then you will be known and you will know that you are the sons of the Living Father."

Now it is my turn to put some challenging questions to you: Do you expect him whom you call Jesus Christ to be a Christian? Now that he is arriving and has arrived, do you expect him to kneel in front of pictures and statues of a dead body that is supposed to represent him nailed on a cross? Do you expect him to pray to himself or to listen to any preaching in the name of the Father, the Son, and the Holy Ghost? And if he cannot be such a Christian, how can you be such a Christian? How can you put mediators and all the distance of your worship between you and him, and still obey his instruction that we be one in him?

Let us be serious in these matters. That cycle has ended. We must start all over again. And we must start from the *Aleph*: "Tell me what Aleph means."

Too many of our people are being led astray by a sentimental teaching that brotherhood means being part of a collectivity. This is not going forward toward the state of oneness (the one individuality). It is falling backward into some form of group souls.

Today as yesterday, the apparition-nonapparition of the Rabbi is a flow of energy that compels us to be other than what we imagine ourselves to be. A spiral has made its turn. If everything must begin again, let it be a real beginning. Let it be a beginning in terms that are totally new, and let the new and the now declare the old to be its opposite.

Consider the spiral—a spiral staircase, for example. In turning, it goes in an opposite direction. Perhaps that illustration makes it easier to understand that our supposed god has become evil, and our supposed evil has become good. And it is in this understanding that we now come to Judas.

Judas is one of my reasons for being in this world. You will never receive "Jesus" if you don't receive "Judas." It is Judas who is on the cross. The passion is his. The traitors are those who mis-translated the Gospels from the Greek and used the word *betray* to describe his "handing over" of the Light to the Darkness. There was no betrayal. This so-called "son of perdition" (John 17:12) who is imagined "damned" (as if the word *damnation* has any sense or meaning at all!) is one of the fundamental aspects of Cosmic Energy—the aspect of its penetration into the existing world where it "loses" itself in a process of degradation.

It is Judas who lives in psyches today. Psyches today do not want *Aleph* to kill their psychological structures. And it is Judas who plants guilt feelings in them. For psyches today, the Passion of Jesus is only a screen. Their real passion is the Passion of Judas.

So the return today is not the return of the Rabbi. What we find ourselves living now is the return of Judas. Judas is the active agent for the penetration of cosmic life in us. The number 30 that is associated with Judas has nothing to do with the 30 pieces of silver reported in our current Bibles. 30 is the number of *Lammed*, by which *Aleph* acts in the flesh.

According to the New Testament, the Rabbi and his apostles acted somewhat as commandos do in a territory that must be conquered. They all charged ahead in the attack even though one of them had to be left behind in the enemy camp, in the shadows of the unconscious. That one was Judas, who was willing to bear the most agonizing pains without being able to die.

Judas entered the psyches. All of the suffering of those who have rejected him who is *in* the Rabbi is his suffering. But with the Second Coming today, the psyches explode.

And Judas? Mission accomplished!

Chapter 28

THE CYCLE OF ABRAHAM

WHEN THE TESTAMENT OF AN ANCIENT, SUB-merged civilization was brought down from the legendary Mount Ararat to the purified plains, its message split in two.

In the East, the *Aleph* shone in a mythical heaven. Hypnotized in their devotion, the people meditated. This was Brahma: *Bayt, Raysh, Hay, Mem, Aleph.*

In the West, the *Aleph* penetrated into Hebrew flesh. This was Abraham: *Aleph, Bayt, Raysh, Hay, Mem.*

These are two contrary and complementary processes. The *Aleph* at the end of Brahma and the *Aleph* at the beginning of Abraham created two entirely different traditions.

In the Orient, the omnipresent *Aleph* ages on the Tree of Knowledge, dries up, decays, and is replaced by another fruit of exactly the same pattern on the same tree.

In the Occident, the *Aleph* dies; its fruit falls on the soil, rots, releases its seed, and produces a new tree. It is a succession of deaths and births.

Abraham was born in Ur of the Chaldees, the light of the magicians. The divine Immanence gave him the order: "Leave this country! Go *Lekh Lekha*, into yourself, into the world of conflicts!" (Genesis 11, 12).

Abraham went, carrying in himself the unmanageable Immanence that is the creator and destroyer of new structures that grow old and go bad and fall and are replaced by new structures that grow old and go bad and fall, indefinitely on and on and on.

Has this cycle now ended? No, we are only in the beginning of its end. Can we disentangle being from newer-ending conflicts? Can we now be—each one according to his or her ability—*in* the Return of the universal Cosmic Consciousness?

Listen to it! It knocks from all directions against the barriers of time, against the prisons of space.

Can we be *in* the Rabbi?

As an incarnation of the Cycle of Abraham with its beginning and ending, the Rabbi remained buried for two days—for 2,000 years of our time. In other words, this event has been 2,000 light-years of our consciousness. The Rabbi's resurrection takes place in the dawn of the third day, the third millenium.

Chapter 29

THE EIGHT PROPOSITIONS

I AM ONLY HALFWAY THROUGH MY BOOK. I MEANT it to be a rather short epistle, and not so personal. I intended to limit myself to eight propositions. They would be simple to understand but so difficult to live that the experience and operation of them would require the personal incarnation of the Rabbi—being *in/as* him and proving it.

"And when he was demanded of the Pharisees, when the kingdom of God should come, he answered them and said, The kingdom of God cometh not with observation: Neither shall they say, Lo here! or, lo there! for, behold, the kingdom of God is within you" (Luke 17:20-21). And this would be the keynote of the New Era. Here are the eight propositions:

1. Seek your total individuality. Don't write it down anywhere. Don't give it a name. Any definition of yourself is a deceptive hideout.

2. You will not find your total individuality. It is your total individuality that sees you, that witnesses your doings. It acts in our space-time continuum but is not restricted to it.

3. Your total individuality is your soul. It abides in the indeterminate plurality of universes. Because it is alive, it is evolving. Because it is outside of time, its evolution is only the time that you need to permit it to find you. Because it is multidimensional, it contributes to the composition of an Ecclesia. It is one and innumerable.

4. Your soul will not find you as long as your consciousness is made of the stuff of false evidences created by your

mind: as long as you do not feel a sense of suffocation in those space-time false evidences.

5. The death of false evidences is a psychological death, announcer of resurrection. Each false evidence denounced opens a window in the inner space where the measurable dies.

6. This death of the measurable in the inner space is a personal experience. All that is said to you about it will prevent it from occurring. Do not listen to the professionals of any religions.

7. Beyond this death, our infinitely multiple individuality reveals to our present person that we are only one of its multifarious manifestations. We then meet the other manifestations of our soul spread out through history, still present and alive.

8. So this consciousness emanating from our soul integrates its earthly past and also its future. It knows itself continuous, without limits. It is all-consciousness, it penetrates every consciousness, it understands every consciousness, and that understanding is love.

REFLECTIONS ON THE
FIRST PROPOSITION

> *Seek your total individuality. Don't write it down anywhere. Don't give it a name. Any definition of yourself is a deceptive hideout.*

Frequently young children remember events that apparently have not taken place here. Sometimes they seem to live in other worlds that we are not aware of and call fictitious. Such youngsters may carry on conversations with invisible beings.

Parents tend to scold them: "Don't talk nonsense." Or they become concerned: "The child is not normal." The fact is that those children are not yet completely embodied in the flesh. They are not completely "born."

Birth is not complete when the baby's body comes out of the womb. Total birth does not come at the moment of physical birth. Birth is a process that prolongs itself when it can, as it can, and in circumstances that are always adverse, no matter what the environment.

Blessed are those whose birth never ends, even if they live to more than one hundred years. (According to some traditions, the complete human cycle is fulfilled at the age of 7 x 12 = 84 years: the seven anciently known planets circuiting along the twelve signs of the zodiac. If that is so, it would even then be only one turn of a spiral. Maturity is an endless ascent.) To prevent oneself from being totally born—to be newborn every "now" moment—is to enter into an infinite process of ripening, or maturing. An endless birth and an endless ripening—can we do it? It may sound contradictory in words, but it is not in fact.

A "completed" birth and a "completed" ripening would come to a stop, unable to proceed any further. They would be confined to a finite state or condition within a limited space-time continuum. Nothing further would be left for them but decay. Still, something must achieve and fulfill itself in a lifetime if that life is more than existence between the birth of a body and its death. Fulfilling is the ceaseless and desperate search for one's total individuality—without ever finding it. Is that a paradox? Think it over. Whenever I try to outline what my real individuality is and fail to do so, I escape a pitfall that would have trapped me. When I escape a final definition of myself, I joyfully exclaim: "I am not *only that!*"

Unfortunately it has become the custom to "orient" our children by means of tests. They are forced to pass through scientific filters, so to speak. The system is that of the computer: it presents only two options—yes or no. According to the results of these tests, the child is classified as "scientific," "literary," "fit only for manual labor," et cetera.

The "orientations" classify young beings so as to adapt them to functions that will—theoretically—allow them to "survive" in a world that is out of control. They don't survive; they quickly become practically dead. Their real creative power has not been given a chance. Hence, the world gets even more out of control. A vicious circle has been set in motion.

Everybody knows it, but what is to be done? The general answer is, "Man does not live by bread alone." So, in clamor and confusion, here comes marching a confused army of promoters and propagandists of doctrines, creeds, and ideals—political, moral, and religious. Fans of "so-and-so" or "such and such" proclaim their leaders to be the holiest and most exalted. And crowds of practically dead, computerized people cheer their slogans.

The world is falling to pieces, and every piece has its fragment of collectivity. Some shave their heads, others grow long hair. Some wear long robes, others wear tight jeans. Each group has its own set of words. The members are glued together by their words. They repeat the same words endlessly. All fresh, new thinking is banished in favor of a collective language limited to the group.

Currently there is a strong attraction for anything that is "collective." I warn you against it. I also warn you against what is spreading everywhere under the name of "creative collectivity." The Chinese now find this "creativity" by following Mao's thoughts without an original thought of their own. By so doing *en masse*, they solve many so-called practical problems with simple means—problems that we think need our most advanced technology. Now we hear people who have visited China advocating similar disciplines that would allow us to accomplish the same results. And the masters of such disciplines exclaim triumphantly, "Look at the ants, worms, and bees! Consider their stupendous organizations, their traffic and transportation systems, their methods of ventilation and air conditioning!"

Alas! Worms, ants, and bees have survived millions of years. No doubt they will still be here after all human beings are gone. But such survival is based and established upon the murder of the Spirit!

Collective creativity tends to destroy the inner life in us. Creativity that is applied merely to concrete, material problems cannot permit that new Life to penetrate our psychological structures. On the contrary, it reinforces those structures by giving them as a goal the very abyss we must avoid at all costs. The trap of the collective is the final contribution to the destruction of our world.

Perhaps it would be useful to think of our small planet as it rolls in its galaxy among billions of other galaxies, incorporating billions and billions of solar systems. Perhaps it would also be useful to keep in mind always that as microbes in these vast spaces, our time is real only for us. And finally, we might observe that we are endowed with a consciousness that can have access to the whole, unlimited ensemble of universes. That consciousness is capable of realizing itself as such and of overthrowing all of its limitations.

142 / *Carlo Suarès*

We can then know—not as belief or creed, but as a certainty and understanding—that we are in this world with no way to escape except through the needle's eye of our psychic cell. It is by this process—"Satan" in its full cabalistic meaning—that through us the cosmic Consciousness finds its freedom and reaches that which is at stake in the entire Creation: the Principle of Indetermination.

Every time we refuse to define ourselves, to be pinned down in any condition or to identify ourselves with it or as it, we are already opening up to the living Eternal, the living Timelessness.

REFLECTIONS ON THE SECOND PROPOSITION

> *You will not find your total individuality. It is your total individuality that sees you, that witnesses your doings. It acts in our space-time continuum but is not restricted to it.*

This proposition proceeds from the first proposition and reveals its contradiction. How can I look for something (my total individuality) when I do not know what it is I am looking for? And why look for something that I cannot find? The answer is given in Genesis 2:18-24. After having projected a prototype of centrifugal Energy (the male Adam), YHWH-Elohim shows him all creatures and asks him to name them. Adam gives them names, but recognizes them as inferior states of energy. He does not find in them a definition of himself.

In the same way today, we are shown all sorts of entities as a test to discover if we identify ourselves with them. Like Adam we give them names. But unlike Adam, we fall into the trap of accepting them as real entities. Then we identify ourselves with those faked entities. We identify ourselves as man or woman, black or white, American or European and we declare that we have a Christian or Jewish, conservative or liberal, cultured or uncultured consciousness. How many descendants of famous historical families think and act just like their ancestors instead of finding their true selves?

Thus false, specious personalities are established and presented for acceptance. They cannot be considered as nothing. But they must be recognized as what they really are. They must be "named" in the cabalistic sense. In other words, we must understand what energy they are made of and classify them properly in the category of prototypes that run counter to Paul's declaration in II Corinthians 5:17: "Therefore if any man be in Christ he is a new creature: old things are passed away; behold all things are become new." Then comes the hour when we must make our choice between the new and the old, the real and the unreal.

To free consciousness from that which limits it is not easy. The old has a gravitational attraction. It also offers an unlimited range of agitations that we call worthwhile activities. We can keep very busy and feel very important when we get caught in such high-sounding words as freedom, justice, democracy, the state, God, et cetera.

It is not easy to see that most of the words that are creating our present chaos have no substance. It is not easy to understand that the words we use to define ourselves have no real meaning. It is difficult to think right through them. And when we do, we may find ourselves in a black tunnel. But in that tunnel, it can happen that we are "called" by a timeless immanence. We are called by our secret name. And when that name is revealed to us, we know ourselves as not knowing *who* we are and never knowing *what* we are. But our multidimensional soul has testified for us. Our total individuality has found us.

REFLECTIONS ON THE THIRD PROPOSITION

> *Your total individuality is your soul. It abides in the indeterminate plurality of universes. Because it is alive, it is evolving. Because it is outside of time, its evolution is only the time that you need to permit it to find you. Because it is multidimensional, it contributes to the composition of an Ecclesia. It is one and innumerable.*

The word *soul* suits this proposition only if the reader will accept the meaning of soul as it is presented here. You must not confuse it with definitions given by theologies that discuss it in the abstract, or by psychologies that deny or limit it. Rather, you must let your soul come forth and define itself.

The world is full of people who are under the illusion that they have been "called." In such a state, they imagine that they have a missionary dictate, a divinely appointed authority. They rush around madly, trying to convert everybody in their path. "I have the truth! All others are heathens!"

We all know the misdeeds of such fanatics. "God told me to do this! God orders you to do what I say!" The Bible is full of such incidents. Most apostles, prophets, swamis, gurus, sages, and so-called saints are defeated by my first proposition. They want to be or become somebody. They want to name and identify themselves. They are stuck in their own revelations.

Your first and most dangerous enemy is your revelation, if by some misfortune you have one. It is not you but your soul that must act. To repeat the essential statement, you will never find or know your total individuality or soul by searching for it. Your aim must be to allow it to find you and flow through you. It will not flow through you if you try to name or describe it—even though you call it God. To name it is to limit it. In a way, you must resist it. You must fight against it as Jacob fought against God and was blessed because he prevailed (Genesis 32:24-30). We must experience that fight and live far beyond the mere symbol of it.

Whatever it is that we call "God" chooses some people as targets and attacks them aggressively. There is nothing that we can do in order to be chosen or not chosen. When it happens, we do not know our fate, but we do know that it will have a great influence on humanity. Its significance will be both individual and collective. It will destroy obsolete structures. It will be revolutionary in the real sense of that word.

Let me once more emphasize that in matters of religion we must never use the same old words that have been taught for generation after generation even though nobody knows what they really mean. We must be very careful about voicing messages that we receive from "beyond." More often than not, they are only projections of our own thoughts in disguise. For the most part they come from the me who, like the big bad wolf in *Little Red Riding Hood*, disguises himself as Grandma. Oh! Jonah, who did not want to be a prophet! The Rabbi always had him in mind.

The only thing that we can really do is to put ourselves at the service of our natural talents. If we do so without exploiting our talents for personal profit (and most people do exploit their talents for personal profit), then those talents are at the service of the Timeless Energy, which is their origin. By becoming their humble servant, we open up channels that Soul will use. Gradually we discover much more in us than we knew we had—more intelligence, more capacities, more inner gifts, and wider horizons. Our soul prospers, growing richly and vigorously. It grows and grows and grows. It wants to grow until it catches fire!

So let us never limit ourselves to what the environment has made us. If it has turned us into a janitor or sales clerk or corporation president or artist, let us realize that we could just as well be a plumber, movie actor, philosopher, or healer. The more open our viewpoint, the greater our soul's harvest.

Do not seek God. Do not pray for miraculous intercessions. Do not be as ice invoking fire. Do not use up potential energy on personal ambitions. Soul is enough. And do not say that Soul cannot die: we can murder it. But we can also nourish it. And if and when soul does take fire, it unites itself with other fires, and those with others and others in an imperishable Ecclesia. This is the omnipresent Reb YHSHWH.

Jesus said, "I have cast fire upon the world, and see, I guard it until it (the world) is afire" (*The Gospel According to Thomas*, L. 10).

REFLECTIONS ON THE
FOURTH PROPOSITION

> *Your soul will not find you as long as your consciousness is made of the stuff of false evidences created by your mind: as long as you do not feel a sense of suffocation in those space-time false evidences.*

We are the meeting place of an indefinite number of universes. Thus we have an indefinite number of bodies. These bodies coexist. They penetrate each other, both in this so-called space-time universe and also in other universes that the personal mind cannot enter because of its sensual origin and beliefs. To that mortal mind, the only reality is this world as it appears to our physical senses. When that mind is told that other worlds exist, it either denies the truth of that statement or thinks of the other worlds as "somewhere else." It always places them "out there" and definitely *not* "here." This belief in a "somewhere else out there" has two different aspects, depending upon one's background and traditions:

1. In the East, it has created the dogma that our daily world is only an illusion. And if it is only illusion, there is no reason to try to change or improve it. We might just as well stay imprisoned in the condition into which we are born. It is by accepting our role that even the lowest of underdogs will supposedly fulfill their function as an element of the Cosmic dream. We need not comment upon a social order built upon such static layers. It is already being destroyed by the Rabbi's fire.

2. In the Jewish-Christian tradition, the belief in a "somewhere else" heaven is constantly splitting our heads, beating unmercifully at reason and common sense. It is wise, and it is crazy. God is supposed to be all-powerful and all-loving, but He has never been able to cope with the evil devil. Evil has appeared in so many shapes, dimensions, moods, and nationalities that we must once and for all admit that that "God" is a delusion. Either that, or we have got to believe that our psyches are only dreaming the blows they receive from this Cosmic Life.

In brief, we are all asked to choose between the reality of a dream or the dream of a reality! Some people advocate an ecumenical combination of these two aspects, as if two errors joined together could make truth!

Billions and billions of words have been written and spoken and taught and fought over for century after century in an effort to cover up the fact that the human race is afraid to face the simple truth that it does not know how anything at all happens to exist. The very words *there is* express a total mystery. And the mystery of mysteries is consciousness.

What is the essence of that mystery? I wish to call it "contradiction." All created universes show it forth in their various manifestations. Contradiction is a timeless solution-dissolution in time (if such words make sense). Actually, all is there to exalt us, not to frighten us. Confined within their boundaries, however, our limited minds want exaltations that appeal to their limitations. They would love to be carried away to regions of supreme happiness, but only if they can take the baggage of pebbles they have gathered along the way—the baggage of words they use to define and identify themselves.

Such minds imagine that they need those words in order to be aware of their own existence, in order to feel alive. But to define oneself with words is to limit oneself to a restricted definition, a restricted identity. The limited mind seeks a limited goal, a goal it would do best not to seek or find.

Among so-called religious seekers for truth, there are endless repetitions of prayers, incantations, liturgies, et cetera. Unless suffocation in words, words, words leads us to break out of such shells, we may die asphyxiated—perhaps quite peacefully. It is the "not thus dying but breaking out" that is our direct opening to Reb YHSHWH, thanks to which we discover that we do not even need him.

REFLECTIONS ON THE
FIFTH PROPOSITION

The death of false evidences is a psychological death, announcer of resurrection. Each false evidence denounced opens a window in the inner space where the measurable dies.

We are surprised and perhaps awed when we discover that our thoughts are living beings. Without always being aware of what we are doing, we give birth to them every moment. Thoughts live their own lives, emanating from us and flying in all directions in search of similar, analogous thoughts with which they unite and coalesce. They traverse the world in an uncontrolled movement, entering into conflict with masses of other thoughts. This tumult falls back upon us. It deprives us of our freedom and carries the world on to an irreversible fate.

The power that is predetermining events is not from eternity: it is merely energy resulting from our own personal doing. If we then take sides in the resulting conflicts, we only intensify the chaos because every one-sided thought breeds its opposite. Both sides are creations of the imagination—of imaginary existences that seem to be real. As responsible adults, our duty is to denounce and deflate these hallucinations. The only way to accomplish this is to think every thought through right to its end in order to unmask every false bit of evidence. This is not easy. The structure of our minds is made of unexplored ideas about everything. So far we have merely taken them for granted and have accepted them because they satisfy us emotionally.

Do you need an example? Let us take two words: *Love God*. Can anybody tell you what those words really mean without trapping you in mere emotional fervor or blind faith? Total understanding is needed in order to dissect from *Love God*, a belief that one may hold more important than his or her very life.

The road to "salvation" always ties the self, the me, to the concept that it has of itself, even (or mostly) when that self is making a point of trying to forget itself. To "try" to get rid of the self is to think about the self that you want to get rid of. It reminds me of the famous recipe for making gold: "Stir water in a cup without thinking of a white elephant." From that moment on, one always thinks of white elephants when stirring water in a cup. In the same way, trying not to think about yourself results in thinking more than ever about yourself.

The disciplines involved in personal salvation give great peace to the soul, but that peace is the peace of anesthesia. When we see that our very notion of perfection is relative because we cannot think "perfection" without comparing it to "imperfection," we shut and lock the last door of evasion from truth.

Here I must say a few words about philosophers. Their jargon takes refuge in abstractions that protect them from everything that is not in their philosophical worlds. Are philosophers thus sheltered from the great sufferings of the masses? Or are they as night watchers, exchanging secrets between themselves in the sleeping cities? I cannot answer those questions honestly. Candidly I confess that I do not understand the language of philosophy. But I venture to suggest that, like the rest of us, philosophers will find truth when they can die to their own words.

There is nothing complicated about my personal experience in this matter. Was it the day before yesterday that I met the Rabbi face to face in Capernaum and was so struck from head to foot that I decided—and still decide—that nothing shall stop me on my way toward the total discovery of all that is to be discovered? In the inner space of my being, which is now wide open, there is nothing left of me that can be measured. I find only a psychological death and an indescribable freedom.

REFLECTIONS ON THE
SIXTH PROPOSITION

> *This death of the measurable in the inner space is a
> personal experience. All that is said to you about it
> will prevent it from occurring. Do not listen to the
> professionals of any religions.*

Every psychological experience is also a physicochemical
operation in a neurophysiological ensemble called "matter." That mass of particles is a field of intra-atomic energy.
Its components act in a double flow, one against the other,
and one for the other. This description corresponds to a
postulate of Cabala, which names these components *Aleph*
and *Tav*, the first and last letters of the alphabet. "In these
two is everything that is," declares the Cabala. *Aleph* represents this double energy as the component called explosive
or timeless. *Tav* is that same double energy, acting as its
"tabernacle" or container; it is the component called "compressive" or "repressive."

Everything that exists can be defined in terms of the
unsettled relationship between those two qualities of the
One Energy. When *Tav* is strongly predominant, the "void"
of the field of battle can be called lead or granite. The *Aleph*
is knocked out with metal or stone. It is buried in the earth,
as is illustrated in the word *Eretz* (meaning earth) when it
is decoded.

Aleph is spelled *Aleph-Lammed-Dallet*. By the action of
its *Lammed*, *Aleph* slowly revives from the knockout.
Starting with the cell (we became acquainted with the cell's
two functions when we analyzed the word *Satan*), it then
climbs the rungs of the biosphere one by one. Thus con-

sciousness gradually becomes aware of the play between explosion and compression. Actually, it is the inner void of energy that becomes aware of the two components by becoming aware of itself. These two components make up the contradictory essence of all consciousness in its action of projecting itself in order to see itself.

It is easy to follow the development of that energy in plants and animals. But when it comes to human beings, our ignorant beliefs in good and evil get in the way and blind us to the truth. These stupid beliefs engender individual and social conflicts. We experience the conflicts and fight wars instead of intelligently learning and understanding the true nature of being.

Tav calls to all that is memory—to all that is repetitious, structured, organized, traditionally established, and set in its ways. It tries to push cosmic energy toward earthly entropy. *Aleph*, on the other hand, aims at the surging forth of the new, the explosion of freedom, the destruction of absolute structures, and the forever birth of the unlimited, undetermined future. *Aleph* is a "conversion" in our psyches of the energy that had structured them and that had been hardening them to a standstill in which no new creative power could come forth. It is this sudden change of direction I call "the death of the measurable" in our inner space. Since it takes place in the "void" of our psychosomatic aggregate, it is a purely individual experience.

This "conversion" restores to cosmic energy the potential that is our true measure. It reverses the thermodynamic law concerning the loss of energy. It permits our individual soul, freshly created, to project in us the same energy that we have given back to the universe. Our physical body will follow its course, end its life, and disintegrate. While it lives, it will be the willing instrument of our new, creative state of being. It will not be the same for our psychical body, because that body is many. We have as many bodies as our soul has. And our soul has as many bodies as we permit it to have—in spheres more and more rarefied and intense. There our limited psychical structures are not admitted.

REFLECTIONS ON THE SEVENTH PROPOSITION

Beyond this death, our infinitely multiple individuality reveals to our present person that we are only one of its multifarious manifestations. We then meet the other manifestations of our soul spread out through history, still present and alive.

Throughout what is called the evolution of the species, the results of *Aleph-Tav* have accumulated as sensory developments and have finally been condensed into an ego perception: "I am." In this process, mountains of information have been constantly received and reacted to by *Aleph* on its way to freedom and by *Tav* in its resistance to freedom. Much in the manner of steam condensing into drops of water, the accumulated data have "condensed" into psychic cells capable of distinguishing themselves from collective consciousness. They now call themselves individual egos, human beings.

However, these egos (the "me" and its human body) are not individuals, as we are inclined to believe. They are packages of collective reactions that constitute the shell, or sentient body, in which the germ of future individuality is born and develops. That germ of future individuality is made of individual, psychosomatic feedbacks moving in directions contrary to the accumulative elements of the shell called "me." That germ of future individuality is a center of energy, developing extrasensory perceptions that are totally independent from the inherited, instinctive reactions of our so-called human species that are considered to be "a step further" in the evolution of the animal species. Finally it breaks that link. (Adam declares that he is not one of them.) Then it is on its way to true individuality if—and only if—it understands clearly that its real life can be found only in the total freedom of *Aleph.*

The mass of research that is being done today in extrasensory perception, thought transmission, metapsychic phenomena, mental healing, and so forth is part of the opening of psyche to energies that are above and beyond everyday consciousness. This is preparation for the Second Coming of the vital flow that started a new era 2,000 years ago. We are already discovering totally new lines of consciousness. And we are learning that, far from hardening the psychic shell, true individuality breaks it to pieces.

The game is now beginning. How are we going to play it? Much depends upon one's condition, and many are in adverse circumstances. Some say that they are overwhelmed with work, exhausted, and suffering too much to even think about these things. I wonder.

I think of a friend who was living in the most appalling conditions in Vietnam. Life had become absolutely impossible. But he began to live what I am trying to explain here, and he came to fulfillment. Was it in spite of or because of his tragic state of affairs?

Come truly to that so-much-talked-about "second birth," and a double vital flow is set in motion between the soul and the personal "me" who is its emanation. That double flow constitutes the real individuality. And when that individuality is born in the soul, it is there forever: it is immortal.

The future of the soul depends upon what its emanation (the "me") has been and has done. If the germ of soul is not allowed to develop, soul cannot constitute itself a whole. It goes back to the group consciousness with which its "me" has remained attached. It can reincarnate in a thousand ways. There are as many different existences after death as there are in this world. But if soul is allowed to grow so that it "catches fire," it links itself to souls of higher and higher "temperatures." Soul is free to choose its "families," call them Christ, Buddha, Krishna, or whatever.

The emanations of this consciousness, one and many, have appeared to us only occasionally in history, but they are ever-present and omniactive. Consciousness finally integrates as Soul—renewed, restored, perfected. Consciousness is One and All.

REFLECTIONS ON THE EIGHTH PROPOSITION

> *So this consciousness emanating from our soul integrates its earthly past and also its future. It knows itself continuous, without limits. It is all-consciousness, it penetrates every consciousness, it understands every consciousness, and that understanding is love.*

The idea of reincarnation, which is so prevalent in some Eastern traditions, is now spreading to the West in simplified forms. Here it is not the result of religious teaching but of practical experience. More and more Westerners are beginning to recall past lives and to remember events that occurred before they were born. Some critics retort that such memories are probably only the result of inherited genes that have been transmitted from one generation to the next. But if those genes and those memories are now part of the living person, surely this is reincarnation. What are the critics objecting to?

At any rate, this argument about the "after death" and "after life" is irrelevant. The future and all theories about such future have nothing to do with the soul that is experiencing the timeless. Linear time as past, present, and future can be likened to fuel whose potential energy can be used or not used. If and when the flash of timelessness meets it, linear time explodes. Then something indescribably different occurs. Nobody knows exactly what, and nobody can describe it. It occurs not only in the individual or in a number of individuals, but in the entire universe.

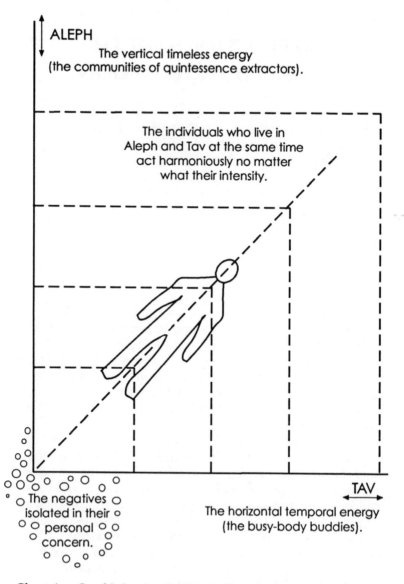

ALEPH

The vertical timeless energy
(the communities of quintessence extractors).

The individuals who live in
Aleph and Tav at the same time
act harmoniously no matter
what their intensity.

The negatives
isolated in their
personal
concern.

TAV

The horizontal temporal energy
(the busy-body buddies).

Chart 4. Combining inspiration with technique—aleph/tav.

We must give all of our being and the utmost of our capacity to this unfoldment. Those who do this soon see that their beings and capacities do not belong exclusively to them. They have been cultivated during generations of successive incarnations—incarnations that still live and coexist in them now. And they can become active in us again as soon as our understanding permits them to do so.

If we look carefully, we see that true "artists" or "geniuses" have abandoned mere desire for fame and fortune. They do not stop after producing one masterpiece or miracle. They are never totally satisfied with their past work. (See Chart 4.) On the contrary, they may be more surprised than anybody else at the excellent results, because all along they have been conscious of constant failure in their efforts, so to speak, to put *Aleph* and *Tav* together. They cannot accomplish a masterpiece through *Aleph* alone (inspiration), nor through *Tav* alone (technique). So at whatever level they are working, they are compelled to be both totally whole and totally cut in half at one and the same time. This is the fantastic adventure of life.

Appendix 1

GNOSTICISM AND DOCETISM

I THINK IT IS IMPORTANT TO REPEAT HERE THAT the Second Coming, or Return of the Rabbi, is a renewed perception of an event that is ever-present. Today that perception must be discussed in the light of our most advanced scientific knowledge. The words of 2,000 years ago were modern in their time, but they are mostly obsolete today. If we insist upon limiting ourselves to those ancient words in their many ancient translations, we fall not only into senseless archaisms but also into hopeless misinterpretations. Thus we lose the vital truths and facts that they were meant to convey and that can and must be lived in the present, in the omnipresence of now.

Gnosticism appears in many writings that just preceded or just followed the canonical Gospels in the New Testament of the Bible. The Gnostics taught that knowledge, more than faith, is the means of salvation. According to their doctrine, all existences originated in God by successive emanations. These they termed eons, and Christ was considered to be only a higher eon.

Most Gnostic writings date from the second century, before the Persian Manichaeus in the third century presented his doctrine concerning separate principles for good and evil. The Manicheistic theology derived from various sources, most notably Paul's nightmares and phobias. Paul's unsolved conflicts between Spirit and flesh led to the assertion by Manicheans that Satan is co-eternal with God. And that theory was a total contradiction of the earlier Gnosticism.

By the third and fourth centuries the fathers of the church, which was still in the process of formation, had already tampered with the Gnostic texts sufficiently to neutralize them so that they would not contradict nor interfere with their church organization.

Any opposition to the church fathers was declared heresy. Even so, such so-called heresies continued to proliferate. When the bishops found themselves fighting on more fronts than they could handle by peaceful means, they resorted to sterner measures. Soon Gnostics, Docetists, Priscillianists, and even Manicheists were being persecuted and martyred. Their books were seized and burned. Everything that did not support the new church theology had to be destroyed and replaced with convenient church formulas.

However, many of the forbidden documents were so popular that they seemed to come to life again from their ashes. Most of them are unknown and unread today, except by scholars who tend to treat them as folklore. There is far more to learn from them than such scholars imagine. The writings reveal that a widespread psychological adventure—confused and chaotic—had begun with the penetration into psyches of the tremendous energy introduced by the Rabbi and his apostles. This energy shattered minds for generations. Of all the scattered pieces of knowledge that can be gathered today, those of major interest here are undoubtedly found in the Gnostic writings. The fragments that remain have been rewritten, often by careless and ignorant scribes. Even so, they have conserved the essence of an extraordinary psychic adventure lived in factual experience.

The Gnostics have been reviled, ridiculed, and repulsed, perhaps because they were not understood. Some Gnostics, such as the Ophites, rediscovered fragments of the original Cabala. Others, such as the Docetists, clearly understood that the appearance of the Rabbi was a metapsychical phenomenon. The Christology of Docetism considers that a descent of the Christ occurred as the appearance of the Rabbi, whose birth, life, and death took place without a truly fleshly embodiment.

Perhaps the Docetists went too far in the negation of physical reality. But there is no doubt that they received the revelation that this world is nothing but the projection of a certain consciousness that at that moment erupted so powerfully in daily consciousness that its brightness obliterated it historically. In other words, they saw clearly that everyday consciousness and its sensorial world had been challenged by a happening that could appear only as a projected image. So they denied its historicity. They found stupendous words to describe the authenticity of this adventure. Some of those Gnostics were geniuses. They left records that are a dazzling aperture to the world of symbols.

Gnostic tradition asserts that the Rabbi returned after his "death" to teach a small group of disciples. The teaching was all the more valuable because it was delivered directly by a non-fleshly being who had come to open his world to us. Gnostics did not identify the situation as live people being taught by a ghost from the world of the dead. On the contrary, they saw the situation as one alive appearing and teaching in our world for the dead. There we touch upon the true event that transformed a belief in a personal Rabbi into divine Power Itself. Thus Docetism opened not only the world of symbols but also a passage between the living and the dead.

The Church violently rejected it. The Church insisted (and still insists) that the Resurrection was that of the physical body, the flesh of Christ. It added that that body had become "glorious" (whatever that may mean), and was carried "up" into Heaven. Thus church doctrine violently bangs the door shut on us, the living, whose fleshly bodies remain in their burial grounds. The genius of the Gnostics left the door open. Today it is still open. Gnostic tradition went underground but has been kept alive through the centuries. Now it is reappearing in full light and has much to say.

The story of Christ and the stories in the Gospels are only what could then be seen, recorded, and understood (or misunderstood) by minds unable to cross the threshold of linear time. To such limited minds, including those today that remain imprisoned in the boundaries of linear time, all that is beyond human reason seems abstruse, secret, occult, esoteric, mysterious, or supernatural. The world of truth is not revealed to or by human reason. Beyond such reason, all is seen as normal and natural, whether understood or not. In truth, nothing at all can ever be grasped by the limited, so-called thinking mind.

Whatever it is that we call Christ (if we care to use that word) is far more than the historical personage to whom that title is generally attributed. Christ is identical with Cosmic Energy.

The cross is no longer the miserable instrument of torture so fearfully spoken of everywhere. It is *Tav*, the universal resistance to the universal Life that opposes itself to itself and limits in time that which can never be limited. Thus the sublime totality of consciousness sees itself through its nonconsciousness.

Appendix 2

G. R. S. MEAD

GENERALLY SPEAKING, THE 19TH CENTURY oriented minds to material concepts of the universe, human beings, and everything else. This triumph of matter was hailed as rational enlightenment. Karl Marx, its prime prophet, called upon all to bow down and worship matter. He was responsible for the myth of "objectivity." History became merely a material process limited to linear time. But while the doctrine of materialism was being noisily established, a totally different trend of thought that did not agree at any point with Marxist dogma also came forth. Compared to Marx's enormous success, it had few followers.

Mme. H. P. Blavatsky founded the Theosophical Society in 1875. Hers was the first serious attempt in the West to introduce direct knowledge by psychic means. Its inspiration came from the East. A few great minds gathered around Mme. Blavatsky. Mrs. Annie Besant acquired a certain fame. Others, such as G. R. S. Mead, have been almost forgotten.

Mead produced a great number of important translations and commentaries on the ancient Gnosis. They include *Pistis Sophia, The Gospel and the Gospels*, and *Did Jesus Live 100 B.C.*, published by Watkins in London. Then there are *Some Mystical Adventures* and a series of small volumes numbered 1 to 11, published by The Theosophical Publishing Society (1907–1908): *The Gnosis of the Mind, The Hymn of Hermes, The Vision of Aridoeus, The Hymn of Jesus, The Gnostic Crucifixion, The Mysteries of Mithra, A Mithraic Ritual, The Chaldean Oracles* (two volumes), *The Hymn of the Robe of Glory*, and *The Wedding Song of Wisdom*.

These important works are not the writings of a scholar who attempts to be "objective" by remaining outside of the subject he is reporting. On the contrary, Mead is inside of every word and thought. He is an initiate, enlightening us in depth through the texts that he offers us. His books constitute a revival of Gnosticism. In my opinion, their time has come. They should be exhumed from the dust that covers them.

In an earlier volume[1] I quoted a passage from Mead's *The Gnostic Crucifixion*. Mead gives only a fragment of the original text and follows it with another fragment, *The Hymn of Jesus*. Both fragments are extracted from *The Acts of John*, a collection of texts put together by a certain Leucius (surnamed Charimus) about A.D. 130, before Gnostics were considered heretics.

The Acts of John refers to The Gospel According to St. John in the New Testament of the Bible. According to Mead, it is written in very much the same style. But if the author knew John's thoughts (and the text is written in the first person as if by John), why does *The Acts of John* tell a story so different from The Gospel According to St. John? Why does he contradict himself? The answer is obvious. In the Gospel, John dictated certain episodes from the life of his Master for the benefit of multitudes. But the *Acts* contain the deep teaching intended for a small circle who could understand it. The Gospel is exoteric, the *Acts* are esoteric.

This corresponds to the general concepts of the Gnostics. They always declared that the Gospel narratives are only allegories presenting in pictures of material events that which far surpassed such pictorial form. According to Mead, the Gnosis is pre-Christian, and what is called Gnosticism is really Christianized Gnosis that existed in the time of Paul.

---

[1]Carlo Suarès, *The Cipher of Genesis* (York Beach, ME: Samuel Weiser, 1992).

Although *The Acts of John* is certainly from the second century, it is not found incorporated in any doctrine before that of the Priscillianists in the fourth century. At that time the Iberian Peninsula was flooded with Gnostic documents, despite the fact that church bishops forbade them and did their best to burn them. Gnostics were burned, too. They had become a danger to the church. Here let me quote Mead on a certain Ceretius:

> Ceretius, one of the bishops presumably, had sent Augustine some of the books of these Gnostics; he himself seems to have been inclined to approve them. Augustine, in his answer, picks out for detailed criticism one document only—our Hymn. Concerning this he writes: "As for the Hymn which they say is that of our Lord Jesus Christ, and which has so greatly aroused your veneration, it is usually found in apocryphal writings, not peculiar to the Priscillianists but used by other heretics."
>
> Augustine adds a quotation, from the introduction of the Gnosis M.S. of the Hymn, which runs: "The Hymn of the Lord, which He sang in secret to the holy Apostles, His disciples, for it is said in the Gospel: 'And after singing a hymn He ascended the mount.' This Hymn is not put in the canon, because of those who think according to themselves, and not according to the Spirit and Truth of God, and that it is written: 'It is good to hide the sacrament of the King; but it is honorable to reveal the works of God.' "
>
> The Gospel referred to cannot be either Matthew (XXVI, 30) or Mark (XIV, 26), both of which read, "And when they had sung a hymn, they went out to the Mount of Olives." The second quotation I am unable to trace.[2]

---

[2]G. R. S. Mead, *The Hymn of Jesus* (London & Benares: Theosophical Publishing Society, 1907), pp. 22–23.

Appendix 3

THE HYMN OF JESUS

ACCORDING TO MEAD, ONLY PART OF THIS famous "Hymn of Jesus" was known until a Mr. James published important fragments of *The Acts of John* (translated by Bonnet) in 1899. They had been discovered in a 14th-century manuscript that had been kept in the imperial library of Vienna. Mead adds that the document is unfortunately written by a negligent copyist.

Here is the text, with reservations as to its authenticity (but its quality of heart pleads in its favor):

"Glory to Thee, Father!

Amen!

Glory to Thee, Word (*Logos*)!

Amen!

Glory to Thee, Grace (*Charis*)!

Amen!

Glory to Thee, Spirit!
Glory to Thee, Holy One!
Glory to Thy Glory!

Amen!

We praise Thee, O Father;
We give Thanks to Thee, O Light;
In Whom Darkness dwells not!

Amen!

(For what we give thanks to the Logos).

[Or, if we adopt the "emended" text:
For what we give thanks, I say:]

I would be saved; and I would save.

Amen!

I would be loosed; and I would loose.

Amen!

I would be wounded; and I would wound.
[Or, I would be pierced; and I would pierce.]

Another reading has:
I would be dissolved (or consumed for love);
And I would dissolve.

Amen!

I would be begotten; and I would beget.

Amen!

I would eat; and I would be eaten.

Amen!
I would hear; and I would be heard.

Amen!

[I would understand; and] I would be understood;
    being all Understanding (*Nous*).

[The first clause I have supplied; the last is
    probably a gloss.]

I would be washed; and I would wash.

Amen!

(Grace leadeth the dance.)

I would pipe; dance ye all.

Amen!

I would play a dirge; lament ye all.

Amen!

The one Eight (Ogdoad) sounds (or plays) with us.

Amen!

The Twelfth Number above leadeth the dance.

Amen!

All whose nature is to dance [doth dance].

Amen!

Who danceth not, knows not what is being done.

Amen!

I would flee; and I would stay.

Amen!

I would be adorned; and I would adorn.
[The clauses are reversed in the text.]

Amen!

I would be at-oned; and I would at-one.

Amen!

I have no dwelling; and I have dwellings.

Amen!

I have no place; and I have places.

Amen!

I have no temple; and I have temples.

Amen!

I am a lamp to thee who seest Me.

Amen!

I am a mirror to thee who understandest Me.

Amen!

I am a door to thee who knockest at Me.

Amen!

I am a way to thee a wayfarer.

Amen!

Now answer to My dancing!

See thyself in Me who speak;
And seeing what I do,
Keep silence on My Mysteries.

Understand, by dancing, what I do;
For Thine is the Passion of Man
That I am to suffer.

Thou couldst not at all be conscious
Of what thou dost suffer,
Were I not sent as thy Word by the Father.
[The last clause may be emended:
I am thy Word; I was sent by the Father.]

Seeing what I suffer,

Thou sawest Me as suffering;
And seeing, thou didst not stand,
But wast moved wholly,
Moved to be wise.

Thou hast me for a couch; rest thou upon Me.

Who I am thou shalt know when I depart.
What now I am seen to be, that I am not.
[But what I am] thou shalt see when thou comest.

If thou hadst known how to suffer,
Thou wouldst have power not to suffer.
Know [then] how to suffer, and thou has power not to
 suffer.

That which thou knowest not, I Myself will teach thee.

I am thy God, not the Betrayer's.

I would be kept in time with holy souls.

In Me know thou the Word of Wisdom.

Say thou to me again:

Glory to Thee, Father!
Glory to Thee, Word!
Glory to Thee, Holy spirit!

But as for Me, if thou wouldst know what I was:
In a word I am the Word who did play [or dance]
all things, and was not shamed at all.
'Twas I who leaped [and danced].

But do thou understand all, and, understanding, say:

Glory to Thee, Father!

Amen!

(And having danced these things with us, Beloved, the
    Lord went forth. And we, as though beside our-
    selves, or wakened out of [deep] sleep, fled each
    our several ways.)[1]

---

[1]G. R. S. Mead, *The Hymn of Jesus* (London & Benares: Theosophical
Publishing Society, 1907), pp. 22–23.

Appendix 4

THE VISION OF THE CROSS

1. [97 (xii.)] And having danced these things with us, Beloved, the Lord went out. And we, as though beside ourselves, or wakened out of sleep, fled each our several ways.

2. I, however, though I saw the beginning of His passion, could not stay to the end, but fled unto the Mount of Olives weeping over that which had befallen.

3. And when He was hung on the tree of the cross, at the sixth hour of the day darkness came over the whole earth.
    And my Lord stood in the midst of the Cave, and filled it with light, and said:

4. "John, to the multitude below, in Jerusalem, I am being crucified, and pierced with spears and reeds, and vinegar and gall is being given Me to drink. To thee now I speak, and give ear to what I say. 'Twas I who put it in thy heart to ascend this Mount, that thou mightest hear what disciple should learn from Master, and man from God."

5. [98 (xiii.)] And having thus spoken, He showed me a Cross of Light set up, and round the Cross a vast multitude, and therein one form and a similar appearance, and in the Cross another multitude not having one form.

6. And I beheld the Lord Himself above the Cross. He had, however, no shape, but only as it were a voice—not, however, this voice to which we are accustomed, but one of its own kind and beneficient and truly of God, saying unto me:

7. "John, one there needs must be to hear those things, from Me; for I long for one who will hear.

8. "This Cross of Light is called by Me for your sakes sometimes Word (Logos), sometimes Mind, sometimes Jesus, sometimes Christ, sometimes Door, sometimes Way, sometimes Bread, sometimes Seed, sometimes Resurrection, sometimes Son, sometimes Father, sometimes Spirit, sometimes Life, sometimes Truth, sometimes Faith, sometimes Grace.

9. "Now those things [it is called] as towards men; but as to what it is in truth, itself in its own meaning to itself, and declared unto Us, [it is] the defining (or delimitation) of all things, both the firm necessity of things fixed from unstable, and the 'harmony' of Wisdom.

10. "And as it is Wisdom in 'harmony,' there are those on the Right and those on the Left—powers, authorities, principalities, and demons, energies, threats, powers of wrath, slanderings—and the Lower Root from which hath come forth the things in genesis.

11. [99]. "This, then, is the Cross which by the Word (Logos) hath been the means of 'cross-beaming' all things—at the same time separating off the things that proceed from genesis and those below it [from those above], and also compacting them all into one.

12. "But this is not the cross of wood which thou shalt see when thou descendest hence; nor am I he that is upon the cross—[I] whom now thou seest not, but only hearest a voice.

13. "I was held [to be] what I am not, not being what I was to many others; nay, they will call Me something else, abject and not worthy of Me. As, then, the Place of Rest is neither seen nor spoken of, much more shall I, the Lord of it, be neither seen [nor spoken of].

14. [100 (xiv)]. "Now the multitude of one appearance round the Cross is the Lower Nature. And as to those

whom thou seest in the Cross, if they have not also one form, [it is because] the whole Race (or every Limb) of Him who descended hath not yet been gathered together.

15. "But when the Upper Nature, yea, the Race that is coming unto Me, in obedience to My Voice, is taken up, then thou who now hearkenest to Me, shalt become it, and it shall no longer be what it is now, but above them as I am now.

16. "For so long as thou callest me not thyself Mine, I am not what I am. But if thou hearkenest unto Me, hearing, thou, too, shalt be as I [am], and I shall be what I was, when thou [art] as I am with Myself; for from this thou art.

17. "Pay no attention, then, to the many, and them that are without the mystery think little of; for know that I am wholly with the Father and the Father with Me.

18. [101 (xv.)] "Nothing, then, of the things which they will say of Me have I suffered; nay that Passion as well which I showed unto thee and the rest, by dancing [it], I will that it be called mystery.

19. "What thou art, thou seest; this did I show unto thee. But what I am, this I alone know, [and] none else.

20. "What, then, is Mine suffer me to keep; but what is thine see thou through Me. To see Me as I really am I said is not possible, but only what thou art able to recognise, as being kin [to Me] (or of the same Race).

21. "Thou hearest that I suffered; yet I did not suffer: that I suffered not; yet I did suffer: that I was pierced; yet was I not smitten: that I was hanged; yet I was not hanged; that blood flowed from me; yet it did not flow: and in a word the things they say about Me I had not, and the things they do not say those I suffered. Now what they are I will riddle thee; for I know that thou wilt understand.

22. "Understand, therefore, in Me, the slaying of a Word (Logos), the piercing of a Word, the blood of a Word, the wounding of a Word, the hanging of a Word, the passion of a Word, the nailing (or putting together) of a Word, the death of a Word.

23. "And thus I speak separating off the man. First, then, understand the Word, then shalt thou understand the Lord, and in the third place [only] the man and what he suffered."

24. [102 (xvi.)] And having said these things to me, and others which I know not how to say as He Himself would have it, He was taken up, no one of the multitude beholding Him.

25. And when I descended I laughed at them all, when they told Me what they did concerning Him, firmly possessed in myself of this [truth] only, that the Lord contrived all things symbolically, and according to [His] dispensation for the conversion and salvation of man.[1]

[1]G. R. S. Mead, *The Gnostic Crucifixion* (London & Benares: Theosophical Publishing Society, 1907), pp. 12–19.

Appendix 5

❧

THE GOSPEL ACCORDING TO THOMAS

IT WILL SOON BE UNDERSTOOD AND ACKNOW-ledged that the Christian Era is the result of the bursting of the Jewish shell 2,000 years ago— of the destruction of Jerusalem and the appearance and violent expansion of the contents of that shell: Israel incarnate and the Apostles. The apostles made their way all over the world. They were bearers of the torch that the Rabbi had set on fire. They created an extraordinary tumult in the minds of multitudes— an uproar, a confused and excited psychological state.

A Cosmic Energy that had been unknown until then invaded humanity. It irrupted in all lands from the Near East to the extreme north of Scandinavia, from Spain to India and the heart of Africa. I am not referring only to historical events, although they have been and still are today on a scale of violence carried to the maximum intensity that any epoch can endure. I am rather considering the psychic commotion, accelerated fury, and amplified magnitude of the tragedies that drive our half-animal species toward its mutation: the birth of Adam.

Time has been shaken out of a slumber that has lasted so many centuries. It is now self-generating its acceleration. Its momentum tends toward a limit that cannot but shatter the structures of its dreams. Everybody feels that this is bound to happen. We cannot rely on any documentation concerning how it began in the first centuries of our era. The true information was all accumulated in Alexandria, and was later systematically burned and destroyed. Today we have mostly delirious hagiographies in which incredible miracles and fantastic deeds are told of every one of the Apostles.

Texts, or rather fragments of texts, are still available in Aramaic, Greek, Coptic, and other idioms. Most of them have been rewritten, recopied, and meddled with by ignorant and primitive scribes who enjoyed them as children enjoy fairy tales. They repeat stories that were told verbatim in Spain, Egypt, Persia, and Rome about a miraculous being whose apparition became more and more legendary as the years passed.

The fathers of the church considered them to be "mud," but a number of bishops thought that some "fragments of gold" could be found in them. What they called gold were obviously the doctrinal elements that appear in places. Our view is different. And our task is more difficult because, even when we deal with texts established by scholars, we discover that they are generally twisted by the so-called learned people who translated them.

Here is a good example of that in the book published by Jean Doresse, the distinguished French archeologist. In 1945 he discovered *The Gospel According to Thomas* among other documents in an urn in Upper Egypt. Monsieur Doresse then translated this Gospel from the ancient Coptic and added his comments on it, comparing it to the canonical writings and also quoting some apocryphal writings. (Incidentally, let it here be noted that the original meaning of the word *apocrypha* derived from the Greek *apokryphos*, is "hidden," not "false." This latter meaning was given by the early fathers of the church.)

Here, freely translated from the French, is what Doresse made of the incident quoted earlier: "The child Jesus has been given in charge to the school teacher Zachee who wants to teach him the letters of the alphabet. Jesus interrupted him from the start: You who do not know the *A* in its nature, how can you teach to others the *B*? Hypocrite, teach first the *A*, if you know it, then we will believe you concerning the *B*."

This translation does not make sense: *A* and *B* have no "nature." The whole point is missed. In that story, the Rabbi is said to know the original code of the sacred language: an inborn knowledge. I know this to be true. And how could it not be? Before coming into this world, was the Rabbi not in *his* world of cosmic energy, the awareness of its process?

Of all the documents that we still have, *The Gospel According to Thomas* is perhaps the text that most convincingly proves the extratemporal origin of the Rabbi's consciousness. It has been widely discussed and questioned. Who is that Thomas? Can this gospel be considered a true Gospel? When was it written? Is it authentic? Are those logia, which all begin with the words "Jesus said," statements that were uttered by him? And so on and on.

All of those problems belong to exegesis—to historical and archeological studies of the documents, their classification, comparative studies of their wording, and the many erudite considerations of people who look at an object from "outside" of it. But who wrote those words and when they wrote them are irrelevant questions. Their proof is in them as they are. Without doubt the words in these logia reflect a thought that is far beyond the realm of minds limited to the appearances of our world. So we need not discuss whether they come from Jesus: we can safely call their source Jesus.

Several translations of and commentaries on that Gospel have been published in different languages. They have all remained within small circles of "specialists." They have been kept away from a wider public, partly through the influence of the Church and partly because their commentators barely bothered to realize their importance for a complete revision and revival of what the Rabbi does and is for us this very day.

In the following pages I shall be quoting from *The Gospel According to Thomas* as published by Harper & Row (Copyright E. J. Brill, 1959): Coptic text established by A. Guillaumont, Henri-Charles Puech, Gilles Quispel, Walter Till, and Yassah'Abd Al Masih.

I shall quote only a few of the 114 logia, adding my personal meditations as I was reading them. They have no "scholarly" ambition: they are notes taken almost at random in "flashes" as I was living in the Life of the Rabbi. To my mind, that draws the line.

Meditations on a Few Logia

> (L. 2) *Jesus said, "Let him who seeks not cease seeking until he finds, and when he finds, he will be troubled, and when he has been troubled, he will marvel and he will reign over the All.*

He told me: "Do not tarry in the houses of those who, in a single breath, tell you that they seek and that they can teach you. For those who seek, what have they to teach? And those who stop seeking, what have they to teach? And if anyone says: 'I teach because I have found,' ask him, 'Do you reign over all?' "

I said: "Rabbi, how can I seek what I do not know?"

He said: "Seek what can never be found; then you will throw away your findings. In the throwing is the seeking."

So I began to wonder why I was seeking without ceasing to seek, and I saw that I could not find my reasons because I did not know who I was. And looking at myself from the inside, I saw that nothing I was made of was myself, of my own nature. I saw thoughts of others, words, words that were not what they said. I was inhabited by my relations.

I said: "Rabbi, I sought into myself and I found legions. I expelled them because they were facing me as the animals were brought to face Adam, and I knew them and I knew their names so I knew that they were not akin to my very own unknowable mystery. I remained empty unto myself and speechless. And that is how I found you."

He said: "You did not find me. It is I who found you and who have chosen you. In very truth it is you in me that I found, in what is in your own nature to be. It is your own nature that found you and knows you, whereas you cannot find it and know it, as you do not know me as I am; but I know you as you are. And, as you are, seek without ceasing to seek what is not in your nature to be and when you will have thrown away the all of it, in its totality, you will be troubled and you will marvel because the all will be your very self and you will reign over the All."

> (L. 3) *Jesus said: If those who lead you say to you: "See, the Kingdom is in heaven," then the birds of the heaven will precede you. If they say to you: "It is in the sea," then the fish will precede you. But the Kingdom is within you and it is without you.*

He told me: "Behold, I will go away, and the people will say: 'He has gone right up, in the Kingdom of the Father, and He will dwell there, in His Glorious Body until the end of the world.' They will lift their eyes and look at the blue that is so near and at the clouds that are nearer still, and they will see the birds that fly right down to the earth, but for lack of finding me, that will have put me where I cannot be found."

I said: "They will say: 'Did he not say that he is Life, and does not the life come to birth in the depth of the seas?' Let us seek in the depth!"

For a very long time I thought that the word *Kingdom* is difficult to understand. Why does he always speak in riddles? "The Kingdom is like a mustard-seed"; it is "like a woman who bears a vase"; it is "like a woman who puts leaven in the dough"; it is like this and like that; and the more the "like," the darker it becomes.

I said: "And who is it, after all, who reigns? Do you not repeatedly say that it is the Father? So how can 'he who finds' reign?"

He said: "While you were seeking that which was yours and finding that what you had thought was yours was to others; while you were naming those things and thereby expelling them; in the empty spaces that they left in you, as small perhaps as a mustard seed, that you think you do not understand, in those voids, little by little, the Kingdom penetrated in you. Thus, you were unaware of knowing and recognizing the Kingdom, because you only knew and acknowledged the voids it came to occupy. But did I not say that he who finds himself is the All that he rejected for the benefit of his death to himself finds the Kingdom in that death? So the Kingdom is in you and out of you."

> (L. 3) . . . *If you (will) know yourselves, then you will be known and you will know that you are the sons of the Living Father. But if you do not know yourselves, then you are in poverty and you are poverty.*

Had he not said, "First, then, understand the Word, then shalt thou understand the Lord, and in the third place, only, the man and what he suffered"?[1]

I was meditating on those words when I met many people. They were saying: "I know myself; I am proud or meek or avaricious or generous or sensual or chaste or envious or charitable or active or lazy." And I asked: "Are you the incarnation of Pride or Meekness or Greed and so on, in the very nature of those qualities, totally present to themselves in self-awareness?"

Thus I saw that there is a wide gap between knowing and understanding. And I saw that the people who were thus talking were like rusted and broken spare parts of a mechanical device, the use of which had been forgotten. I could not see what it was in them that they qualified as being in or out of one or the other of their "capital sins" or "holy virtues." My meditation then led me to wonder what the Rabbi meant by "knowing oneself," because I fancied that I could only know some thoughts, as they passed swiftly through me, and that none of them could declare, "I am." Thus, when I happen to read words that I have written, I ask: "Who is there to know?"

So, maybe, it is those thoughts—those living beings— who chose me, not I who think them. Maybe they have known me as one who would allow them to pass—as a good craftsman, humble in their manipulation—who allows every word to be complete in its significance. Is it, then, that my words are the knowledge of myself, by which others can know he who has written them and by which

---

[1]See *The Vision of the Cross*, p. 216.

the reader reveals to the writer that he, the writer, is the son of the Living Father? As to the writer, it is obvious that he must first understand the Word, because in the Word is the Lord, and in the Lord there is humanity.

(L. 4) *Jesus said: The man old in days will not hesitate to ask a little child of seven days about the place of Life, and he will live. For many who are first shall become last and they shall become a single one.*

An old man was reading that desperate cry of the Sulamite: "Who will teach you to be for me like a newborn brother not yet depraved by time? I would quench your thirst in the Realms of space and, moreover, do so as a free woman. I would write your incessant beginnings beyond time with my inheritance through the generations. Living together, we would mingle these two streams."[2]

And the old man felt suddenly as a blow in the remotest depth of his being that cry that came from the earliest of early ages, that cry as a reproach, as a condemnation, as an unbearable remorse. He fainted away and fell.

When he woke up, after a period of time that he could not evaluate, he found himself in a room where a newborn child was asleep. And the words of the Rabbi came to his mind: "Ask a child of seven days about the place of Life."

The child of seven days was fast asleep, and the old man, not remembering what had happened to him, tried to seek the timeless arrow that had wounded him, but could not locate his pain, because it had gone. And seeking again, he found, instead of a pain, something as a small flame, flickering shyly, that was hidden somewhere in the heart's region.

He contemplated the child in its peaceful slumber. "I must," he thought, "I must be as cautious as this newborn,

---

[2]From *The Song of Songs* by Carlo Suarès, trans. George Buchanan (Boston: Shambhala, 1972).

for fear that this wavering flame goes out. In this child all the created is yet uncreated and all the possibilities are buried in the forgotten memories. The Powers of the Universe have engraved in this receptive flesh a singular destiny that circumstances will deal with. In very truth, this child is not yet born. . . . May he live old enough to meet his birth!"

And in a flash the old man had a vision of his whole long life, accumulating the alluvions of time, as layers upon layers of sand, of stones, of ruins, of ashes.

"And I am already born," thought the old man. And he smiled.

> (L. 5) *Jesus said: Know what is in thy sight, and what is hidden from thee will be revealed to thee. For there is nothing hidden which will not be manifest.*

People say that when Abram our father received the breath of life and became Abraham, he looked and saw, he listened and heard, he touched and felt, he thought and understood, because he had received the following injunction: "Leave the house of your father; leave the land of your birth; and go *Lekh-Lekha*—towards yourself—in the country that I will indicate." And Abraham, with part of his family, left the land of the Chaldees and led his step toward Canaan, that was the promised land, cursed by Noah.

"Go toward yourself, in the vast universe": that was what I had understood. I walked a very long time, and I finally found myself in a very big city, where I now am, while writing these lines. It is one of those cities where the streets and the street corners are at times under dark skies and at times under highly lighted ceilings. It was the hour when in the big cities spring multitudes of lights of all colors, the hour when compact crowds of those who have done their daily work hurry in confused floods.

I was alone.

And I was meditating, as I always do, by looking at the faces of those passing by. I was also looking at the fantastic scenery all around me that I cannot describe. I see it every day, but it astonishes me every time, and I think of the words of the Rabbi, asking to know what is in my sight so that the hidden is revealed. He probably was mentioning his own presence, facing his disciple, but inside every passerby it was the Rabbi that I was seeing, who—alas—was weeping and lamenting when those faces asserted ruthlessly their "I am."

And I look again at those crowds, those crowds who so long taught themselves to look without seeing that they have ceased to look. They knock each other and squash each other, but they do not see each other. And I, among them, was invisible, and the Kingdom saw them and read the secrets of every one of their faces.

And I thought: the Rabbi is quite right, I must trust appearances. It is my look upon them that I must distrust, because seeing—really seeing—is bringing the Kingdom in: it is communicating. And I thought about all those who shut themselves in, in order to meditate, who sit in isolation and take postures and seek the Kingdom in a silence protected by walls. Alone or in organized groups, those people communicate only with themselves, and find peace of a sort: the peace of their longings.

> (L. 7) *Jesus said: Blessed is the lion which the man eats and the lion will become man; and cursed is the man whom the lion eats and the lion will become man.*

That morning the Rabbi was in a mood to say his parables half jokingly, as he used to, sometimes, when he wanted to convey things that were too serious to be solemn.

And I, laughing: "Rabbi, do you not give the truth in parables, so as to allow people to eat them?"

He answered: "You are mistaken. When the truth is said in words of truth, it appears so simple that he who hears the words says, 'I have understood.' And a while later he says, 'Now I do not understand; how is it that I said I understood?' Because he who says that he has understood only imagines he does, and he seeks not further. Whereas a parable is a riddle and is not understood immediately; therefore, he who hears it seeks. Did you not say that the more I say, 'The Kingdom is like this or that,' the more confused you are? Therefore, you go on seeking."

"But," I said—and I was not laughing now—"did you not say, 'This is my flesh, eat; and this is my blood, drink'?"

And the Rabbi all of a sudden was very angry, and indeed awe-inspiring, as he could be sometimes: "Those who think that they eat my flesh and that they drink my blood, whether in real Presence or in symbol, believe that they are worshiping me, but in truth are cursing me!"

The appearance of the Rabbi had vanished, but the answer to the question that had come to my mind was in me as a vision, clear, simple, and total: an upsetting vision. I saw the persistent and tragic error of absorbing the Spirit day after day, transforming it into matter. I saw the cruel illusion of wanting to uplift oneself toward that which is cast down and destroyed.

The superior energy absorbed (eaten) by the inferior energy is always brought down to the lower levels. And by what countereffect can one imagine going up a ladder thrown on the ground?

I began running in the city, screaming: "Have yourselves eaten by God! Have yourselves eaten by God! People thought I was crazy. I was.

(L. 11) *Jesus said: This heaven shall pass away and the one above it shall pass away and the dead are not alive and the living shall not die. In the days when you devoured the dead, you made it alive; when you come into light, what will you do? On the day when you were one, you became two. But when you have become two, what will you do?*

That which is of the Rabbi is of life and of death. The meaning of those words comes nearer and nearer to their reality when, little by little, we learn to die our life and live our death. Talking about it is calling to contradictory words that confuse minds more than they enlighten them. The Rabbi made use of such contrasts, now petrified in aphorisms. Lives and deaths of all sorts, particularly those that were longing for an "always," introduced into those words their hopes and their blindness: "He has given us an always of life!"

But the Rabbi was not that life preserver. If, out of his compassion, he did happen to comfort some people, he was as a pure, hard diamond when dealing with his disciples.

It belonged to us to ask ourselves: "Am I a living who will not die? But in truth, I feel death set in me. Am I a dead who will not live? But in truth, I feel life set in me."

Those thoughts, and others, came to me whence I know not. They deepened and I plunged in wordless reflections. I felt confusedly, yet with great certainty, that the words of the Rabbi, in their absolute, were the key to whatever I had to say. And I felt a kind of fear as if facing a mystery into which it is not good to investigate.

The words I found and find in the course of history, by means of which I circumvallate myself, can only be those, incomplete, that any epoch uses in the vain attempt to grasp the life that passes. As soon as uttered, they are only old references to alphabetical lists of terms concerning the past. But the Rabbi, although he was perfectly identifiable, in his person, as a rabbi, with all the appearance of that function, emanated such a power that his words, far from running after the flow of time, were always ahead of it. He even taught some of us how to produce an explosion in time by colliding it with timelessness: a process I often mention.

It was then that I decided to always transfer his words in terms of the epochs I happen to reappear in this world. It is very important. The only reality of the passing of time is the passing of words. The people who indefinitely repeat the words that are supposed to have been in use at the time of Pontius Pilate will never be inside the Second Coming. This Coming is the announcement of every day, hour, and minute that will drift through the minds and end in memories. Let the archives of history be archives. They have their place where records are kept. Why do so many people accumulate their pictures in their minds?

The key to them was given by the Rabbi. Open up and let go. Those pictures are dead, and it is tragically true that the dead will not live. But the living will not die: the Rabbi has the awareness of a consciousness that projects itself in what appears as a universe. Then, from that universe, it goes back to itself. It is an instantaneous action, although it appears to us as a duration of billions of years. And that action can well be compared to the "devouring of the dead" that makes them alive. The consciousness buried in its own projection slumbers as one not knowing where it came from. It gradually awakens. In this world of ours, it passes from mineral to vegetable to animal, and suddenly in humans it becomes two.

I feel the two, I meditate upon it. I see that it is the very essence of consciousness. It is aware of itself as a contradiction. I do not shun its conflicts. I do not seek unity: it would be a deadly mistake. I pity those who beg to be led to the One.

The One is twofold. I am the One in Two.

And now what do I do?

Am I astonished to be here, limited and boundless? To be one and two and three and many? To be mortal and immortal?

When your soul acknowledges you and testifies for you, the answers are there.

(L. 75) *Jesus said: Many are standing at the door, but the solitary are the ones who will enter the bridal chamber.*

I said: "You shouldn't say that, Rabbi, you'll have many unfortunate hermits quoting you."

"I know," he said. "They fear the intruder who would step in and marry their soul."

"That," I said, "is really funny."

(L. 56) *Jesus said: Whoever has known the world has found a corpse, and whoever has found a corpse, of him the world is not worthy.*

The Rabbi, in his visible person, is not to our image the emanation of a soul more or less individuated, but a total soul fallen in a body.

Star of Bethlehem . . . symbol of a reality! . . .

Let us stop a while with the striking image of "he who has known the world has found a corpse, and the world is not worthy of him." If the world is not worthy of him, it is because he, in his own consciousness, and speaking in the name of that consciousness, judges that the world he came to explore, that that corpse, belongs to energies of an inferior quality. Those words contradict the Christian mythology, and we are free to accept them or not. They may be the origin of the "Descent of Christ in Hell," a legend that some people evoke sometimes.

In symbolic words whose meaning is beyond the general trend of thought of our epoch, the Rabbi refers to some primordial data of the Cabala, which we discover little by little. His assertions, at times strange and nearly always contradictory, are the outcome of a clear and well-ordered thought, intelligent, intelligible, and monolothic—and, after all, rather simple. I have given its key at the very beginning of these pages and practically on every page.

Need I repeat that the universal Consciousness projects itself in Universes and, awaking to its own awareness, retreats from those projections and gathers unto itself the individuated centers of consciousness that have matured and fructified, having burnt their residues?

However simple that image is, it is correct, and everything that the Rabbi says confirms it. Having come to explore the world, he must necessarily meet a corpse, or rather fall into a corpse; otherwise the exploration would not be complete. He must enter into the extreme depths of the mysterious movement of life, where the movement ceases.

Is he clairvoyant? Does he see the life and death of the cells as we can see them through an electron microscope— enlarged billions of times? Does he see that a cell that dies comes to a stop, appears as a hole, and is eaten up? Or, in his prescience, does he know that he will be worshiped as a corpse (a dead cell) and eaten up?

When the Cosmic Consciousness falls into that corpse, there is no death for it. On the contrary, it is within that corpse that is born the supreme clarity, free of its conditioning. It then leaves the body, not without a certain astonishment at having been there.

Did Jesus "sacrifice himself in order to save humanity?" On the contrary. He came to harvest those who are his (those who can enter into his fire and not be consumed), and to leave this world with them. He said so plainly.

The others, in their ceaseless agitation of their borrowed lives, have made their choice: they play the game of who will devour whom. When, exhausted, they stop and move no more, they die without knowing why and are eaten up without knowing by whom. But, says the Rabbi:

> (L. 60) *You yourselves, seek a place for yourselves in Repose, lest you become a corpse and be eaten.*

On that exhortation we can, can we not, seek that place. But where are we to seek it? "Begin," says the Rabbi, "by eating the things that are dead so as to make them alive. Then you will see."

> (L. 11) *In the days when you devoured the dead, you made it alive; when you come into light, what will you do?*

It is not a question of knowing what we will do after having eaten dead fish, flesh, or fowl! Can we hear those words in the pure context of the Rabbi and of the Cabala? Such questions as "when you come into light, what will you do?" can only be answered by those who, indeed, have come into light, or else they would have no foundation.

The words we must use today to say what the Rabbi said must be clearer than the ones his time allowed. They must belong to psychology more than to symbolism. The dead that we eat are our archaic psychological structures that harden and block the way to the new. We must integrate them, assimilate the sclerotic past, revive it, recreate it. We cannot dismiss it. We can fulfill it, as the Rabbi said that he had fulfilled the Scriptures. And the Light enters into us when we have "eaten ourselves," because, to ourselves, we were the obstacle.

On the way to Light, we are alone. We are "One," says the Rabbi. But what is this Energy in us? What is its name? What is its direction? Where does it come from? Where does it go? Has it a will of its own? A purpose? A destiny?

In terms of the Cabala, which the Rabbi knows so well, this Energy is timeless. Its name is Aleph. Its direction it that of Aleph's return to itself. It comes from the corpse when the corpse has been explored. It goes not and comes not. It lives and does not exist. It burns the appearances. Its destiny is movement and rest.

And now, as we stand One within ourselves in the Sacred One of Aleph, we come to light and, behold, we are two!

I said: "Rabbi, I am in the Light, and you want to know what now, being One, I do when I become Two. I first look at the Two, and I see it. I see Light as being Aleph in its container, the Universe, and I see the Universe as being the Aleph contained in itself. I see that all that is is both a contained and a container, and I am their Life as a movement between the Two, and I rest in its incredible speed."

(L. 106) *Jesus said: When you make the two one, you shall become sons of Man, and when you say: "Mountain, be moved," it will be moved.*

It is a constant error to translate *Ben-Adam* as "son of Man." It is putting oneself in the impossibility of understanding that expression. I have lectured and written so much about it that I will only, in a few words, say that Adam is Aleph-in-Blood (*Dam* means "blood" in Hebrew).

Blood is both a resistance to Aleph and a possibility for Aleph to spring back after the impact. In its idiomatic meaning, Ben is Son, but when read with the code, it means that there is a possibility for us to evolve so as to meet the Cosmic Principle of Indetermination.

So Ben-Adam is an equation in which (when we read it in the way that the Rabbi said it) we can see the total evolution of Humanity and the fulfillment of what we are in our Cosmic function. In declaring himself Ben-Adam, the Rabbi says something tremendous, immeasurable—something that is far beyond any tentative definition of humans, of women and men.

So once again we acknowledge the wisdom of him who said: "First know the Word"—the Word meaning the conscious movement between the inner and the outer life. That intense vibration is the Two becoming One, as it is the One becoming Two. Ben-Adam is the beginning and the end of that which has neither beginning nor end: Timeless time in its own diction and contradiction, an enigma compared to which the famous sphinx is only a crossword puzzle.

The difficulties, torments, and bewilderments of human beings are in our impossible quest for the One, since we are deeply buried in the Two as contradiction. when we desperately attempt to extricate ourselves from that mesh, we fall asleep, dream, and fall back in moving sands. Only from the Two can the One spring forth. The One is immanent in the Two.

The universal Energy is One, and it is Two in manifestation. There never is the One without the manifestation. There is never any manifestation whatsoever that is not in the One. We can express that with two words that have had a great fame but that have no real meaning: there is no Spirit without Matter, and no Matter without Spirit. The two are one.

In terms of consciousness, all that exists is alive and conscious, down to the zero of consciousness attributed to stones. Between that zero and the Infinite of the universal consciousness is the sum of all the degrees of consciousness of all that is. The Rabbi is that consciousness in which there are no separations. The Second Coming, today, is the end of the myths that cut everything in two. The Creator and the Creation are One.

(L. 29) *Jesus said: If the flesh has come into existence because of [the] spirit, it is a marvel; but if the spirit (has come into existence) because of the body, it is a marvel of marvels. But I marvel at how this great wealth has made its home in poverty.*

The Rabbi marvels! (See also L. 2: "He who finds . . . will marvel.") We who admire and marvel are young, alert, new in spirit. Our emotion is joyous and creative. Our expression is often pleasant, quick-witted, impulsive. The solemn image of a pontificating Christ that must be worshiped in mono-tones vibrating under dark cupolas is improper.

But can we, first of all, remember some simple cases of our marveling? We marveled when we discovered in the electron microscope the swarming of cells, the intensity of their life; and we marveled when we were shown pictures of the fantastic galaxies, the novas, the "holes" in space, and so on. We marvel when we find ourselves billions and billions of times smaller than a life, and just as many times bigger than a life.

All that is commonplace. But I ask: do we really marvel? If we do, we marvel at the very existence of a speck of dust, don't we? We marvel because we cannot possibly under-stand how it is that it is. The marveling of the Rabbi, there-fore, is above all the stating that the Aleph is everywhere and *that it is not quantitative!* It is total in every point of the Universe. And considering the human body, he exclaims: "How can that wealth have made its home there?"

My meditations on the One and the Two and the cosmic dwelling of Aleph by Aleph being Aleph led me to the notion of a self-engendered Life of the All. I then wondered at the relationship of Aleph and its container Adam, as persistently mentioned by Ben-Adam, the Rabbi. And it is here that we most marvel when we discover that what is so inadequately called the Spirit is the awareness that Aleph has of itself, in Flesh. In the Rabbi, it is aware of being and aware that its Life is beyond measure! The "limited" marvels to find itself without limits!

That which appears to us as a complete cycle of consciousness—its projection in a Universe, its resurrection in that projection, its return unto itself, the intense vibration between itself and itself—all of that cycle appears to the Rabbi in a flash: *The spirit comes into existence because of the body!*

Reb YHSHWH comes from the "Father" as a Life in search of its existence; finds a body of flesh and a body of brothers, his disciples; gathers his harvest of consciousness in flesh—it is a "fire" in the psyches; brings back to the "Father" his gatherings; and leaves behind him his "secret agent," Judas. The Church from outside and Judas from inside infuse in minds the notion that "some other world" exists, and also a sense of guilt. The guilt (the sin) is the animal origin of the human consciousness. The animal-in-human reacts violently; it becomes more and more aggressive; it spreads all over the world. Its conflicts, its wars, its cruelty, and its crude, immature, unripe, undigested impulses create havoc, devastation, and insecurity everywhere. The time is ripe for the Second Coming. It is called forth.

(L. 112) *Jesus said: Woe to the flesh which depends upon the soul; woe to the soul which depends upon the flesh.*

Those words express dramatically the conflict, impossible to solve, that arises if we do not raise our minds to the level of the Cosmic Energy incarnated in the Rabbi.

Ever since humanity has sought to know what it is (a question that the animals do not ask), the animal consciousness in humans has fought a bewildering battle against an invisible enemy: an enemy that it cannot meet because it is its own negation.

Science can easily state that consciousness is born out of water, because our bodies are mostly made of water with only a few chemical elements added to make them more or less solid. That approach does not solve anything. The fact is that that consciousness has only one purpose—itself; one aim—itself; one function—itself.

We an describe it as belonging to the "conservative" flow of the Cosmic Energy. The other flow is that of the Rabbi: the explosive and symbolic Fire, coming from the "Father" and returning to the "Father." The elements that maintain and recreate the totality of that Energy I have called Souls.

Souls are born out of the nebular mists of the unconscious, the subconscious, the collective responses to information. They come to birth when some individuated drops of consciousness are found in that fog. They come out of the symbolic "Water" and gradually catch "Fire." Then a choice of universes is open to them, and they choose according to their "Name," in terms of their "energic" quality. ("I have chosen you," insists Reb Yhshwh.) Then a link is established between the chooser and the chosen, and the chosen are free to choose their connections in the ever-widening network of the "many in one" in which they have entered.

"My" choice ("I," speaking for anyone of us) depends, of course, upon "my" intensity. If the soul depends upon the flesh or if the flesh depends upon the soul "I" am not free to use "my" quantum of Energy. I think it is rather obvious. "My" maximum Energy will be the result of two utmost energies: the soul's and the body's. (Bob Toben, in his delightful book *Space, Time & Beyond*,[3] presents that equation in a general way.)

---

[3]B. Toben, *Space, Time & Beyond* (New York: Bantam, 1983), p. 109.

The freedom thus obtained goes toward the Cosmic Principle of Indetermination. When it meets those who are in the same regions of freedom, it gathers momentum. That acceleration of the one-in-as-many-as-it-can-muster is already the Second Coming. When it will find its total Power, the Rabbi in flesh will be there.

(L. 79) *A woman from the multitude said to Him: Blessed is the womb which bore Thee and the breasts which nourished Thee. He said to [her]: Blessed are those who have heard the word of the Father (and) have kept it in truth. For there will be days when you will say: Blessed is the womb which has not conceived and the breasts which have not suckled.*

(L. 114) *Simon Peter said to them: Let Mary go out from among us, because women are not worthy of the life. Jesus said: See, I shall lead her, so that I will make her male, that she too may become a living spirit, resembling you males. For every woman who makes herself male will enter the Kingdom of Heaven.*

(L. 15) *Jesus said: When you see Him who was not born of woman, prostrate yourselves upon your face and adore Him: He is your Father.*

(L. 18) *The disciples said to Jesus: Tell us how our end will be. Jesus said: Have you then discovered the beginning so that you inquire about the end? For where the beginning is, there shall be the end. Blessed is he who shall stand at the beginning, and he shall know the end and he shall not taste death.*

(L. 19) *Jesus said: Blessed is he who was before he came into being. If you become disciples to Me and hear My words, these stones will minister to you. For you have five trees in Paradise which are unmoved in summer (or) in winter and their leaves do not fall. Whoever knows them will not taste death.*

Those who have access to the original code of the Cabala will reestablish the words of those five logia in their Hebrew and read them according to their real meaning. Then those logia, put together, will provide a stupendous bird's-eye view of the Hebrew fundamental mode of thought and hence of the Rabbi's.

When read in English, or in any other vernacular, those words don't make sense; or if any sense is given to them, I positively declare that it is the opposite of what the Rabbi is saying. He seems to say, "Happy is the barren woman, who does not fulfill her womanhood." And to Peter, "Don't expel Mary. I will give her a chance of becoming a man. As a woman, of course, she cannot enter the Kingdom." Then, alluding to a Cosmic Father, he declares that He is not born of Woman. Is he attributing a body to that Father?

I included in those strange quotations above a question from the disciples about their "end" and the Rabbi's answer: "Blessed is he who shall stand at the beginning, and he shall know the end and he shall not taste death" (L. 18). Must we understand that the beginning has no end? And finally, in poor words, "Be before being, because you can know five trees" (See L. 19).

I added those logia to the others because my meditation on the meaning of the male and female sexes in terms of Cosmic Energy led me to them. I must first state that the five trees are the five first *Sephirot*, a purely cabalistic classification of "transformers" of Energy. (I trust that my readers will excuse me for not explaining what they mean. This is not a textbook on Cabala, but an informal epistle.)

If we wish to deepen our meditation in the direction of those logia, we must do so with a mind absolutely free from symbols. The binomial male-female has been—and still is—a major topic all over the world. Centuries and centuries of words and billions and billions of words dealing with the feminine—from the animal-like woman to the Exalted Lady, from the whore to the goddesses, from the pride of motherhood to the saintly virgin! But where is the root of the matter? Is it biological, physiological, or psychological? Is it individual or social? In a nutshell: what is sex?

The direct approach to the last question is that male and female are two aspects of the One Energy, and so intimately linked that they appear at times to be interchangeable. How can it all happen, why, and when? Does the Rabbi say that he will operate upon Myriam's sexual organs? I sincerely hope that nobody has ever had such an idiotic interpretation. So what is he going to change into what?

Do you remember the 112th logion? "Woe to the flesh which depends upon the soul; woe to the soul which depends upon the flesh." In the logia we are now meditating upon, he deals with the relationship between body and soul. And where does that relationship take place if not in the psyche?

Remember now what I have said so often—that body and psyche have the same origin (sensorial, animal) and that they follow the same process of development (building their structures and maintaining them to the best of their capacity and strength). I also said that when the psyche reaches its own maturity, it can fulfill itself only by making a U-turn, a conversion that turns its original process of building and supporting a framework into a process of freeing itself from its structures.

The first process is the "female" aspect of Energy; the second is the "male." When this happens, the psyche becomes new every moment. It is creative, spontaneous, explosive. It is no longer in bondage to its memories. It ceases to be repetitive. Its goal is no more its own duration, but it finds a Life of a different quality—timeless and, in truth, without death. Then it becomes aware of its soul, and it discovers this that I will put into one short sentence, which, I hope, will give my readers a wholesome shock: *The soul is born female and fulfills itself male.* The more one meditates on that, the deeper and wider is the understanding of the human search for truth, of its errors and its diversities. In fact, the soul has the privilege of choosing its way, and I am inclined to think that the reversing from female to male is the choice of a small minority. The mass—and particularly the Oriental—is taught to remain female, to fall into a universal slumber of an eternal female parent and to wait for the awakening.

Here I cannot resist quoting the first "Stanzas of Dzyan" from Blavatsky's *Secret Doctrine*.

> 1. The Eternal Parent, wrapped in her Ever-Invisible Robes, had slumbered once again for Seven Eternities.

> 2. Time was not, for it lay asleep in the Infinite Bosom of Duration.

> 3. Universal Mind was not, for there were no ah-hi to contain it.

> 4. The Seven Ways to Bliss were not. The Great Causes of Misery were not, for there was no one to produce and get ensnared by them.

> 5. Darkness alone filled the Boundless All, for Father, Mother and Son were once more one, and the Son had not yet awakened for the new Wheel and his Pilgrimage thereon."[4]

There we are! Let us dream of a sleep in the Mother complex where we rested for a duration in which no time passed by; where we were in the mindless state of the uncreated; where no AH-HI was there to disturb (AH: Aleph alive; HI: Aleph's life confined to existence); where we avoided happiness because happiness breeds misery; but, alas, the Son came and started once again on his wheel of reincarnations.

Of course, there is no Eternal Mother. There is no Father in Heaven, either. don't imagine, those of you who ask Him for your daily bread, that there is a personage to hear you. (And let us note parenthetically that those who ask for daily bread are generally those who already have it:

---

[4]"The Stanzas of Dzyan," from Blavatsky, *The Secret Doctrine*, Vol. 1 (London: Theosophical Publishing House, 1893), p. 55. Modern editions are available from the Theosophical Publishing House in Wheaton, IL.

the really poor know that that "Father" allows them to starve to death.)

So here we come to the notions of "beginning and end." The passing from a state of "Nothingness" to a state of "Creation" is only an empty speculation, a pastime for metaphysicians, or a pill to be taken to stop thinking. ("In the beginning God created . . .") I shall not go into any abstractions. The question is: can we know what is the end of anything in terms of Energy? The answer is: we can. An end is the ceasing of inner movement.

Along that line, a first glimpse of what we are seeking is given in astrophysics. (I am considering this only as a layman.) We are led to think that when a star dies (including its connected worlds), it is reduced to a fantastically small volume having an equally fantastic weight (billions of tons for an infinitesimal size) and such a gravitational power that it appears as a dark hole in space, in which even light is absorbed. Let us therefore imagine that that death happens when the balance between the two-in-one energies, Aleph and Tav, is blotted out of existence by the expulsion of Aleph and the absolute triumph of the compressive Tav. That death becomes a center of death, apt to swallow as a vortex any nearby star.

Contrariwise, galaxies are seen rushing at a terrific speed beyond the speed of light, beyond our space-time continuum. In those systems the Aleph with its fantastic power has so defeated Tav that Tav can no longer contain it. I thus imagine that in those cases Tav is still dead and Aleph immeasurably alive. I also imagine that the result is a "calling" of one to the other, and that Aleph, fully alive, rushes toward the dead Tav. (L. 56: "Whoever has known the world has found a corpse. . . .") I now try to elevate my imagination as much as my mental capacities permit. I see an infinitely complex series of Universes in which Aleph and Tav are in infinitely diverse relationships, between the maximum Tav and the maximum Aleph. I see a perpetual movement in a "nontime," a prodigious vibration of life-death-life-death. And I do not see anywhere any Father or any Mother.

But on our microscopic human scale I see a few people, from Abraham to Reb YHSHWH, identifying themselves with the life of Aleph in them—Aleph-Beith: AB translated Father. And I see enormous masses choosing to think of themselves in terms of creatures, born of a universal Mother. Unknowingly, they chose the way to death.

> (L. 22) *Jesus saw children who were being suckled. He said to his disciples: These children who are being suckled are like those who enter the Kingdom. They said to Him: Shall we then, being children, enter the Kingdom? Jesus said to them: When you make the two one, and when you make the inner as the outer and the outer as the inner and the above as the below, and when you make the male and the female into a single one, so that the male will not be male and the female not be female, when you make eyes in the place of an eye, and a hand in the place of a hand, and a foot in the place of a foot, (and) an image in the place of an image, then shall you enter [the Kingdom].*

Many people say that to "enter the Kingdom" we must become as little children. But that is not enough, for the simple reason that it cannot be done! You can fool yourself into believing that you can become as innocent as a baby again, but the truth is that most people are only perverted children, never having gone beyond being infantile. That is not in any way the U-turn I mentioned earlier! The adventure of being in existence is like being in a tunnel: the issue is ahead. The Rabbi says that when we are *in* him we can remove mountains. If my simile is correct, we can compel the tunnel to make a U-turn, we are always going ahead. I don't know if that makes sense, but that's how I feel it.

What the Rabbi says in this logion is again a reference to the consciousness of the One that makes itself Two so as to perceive itself as One. His sublime words recorded in John: "I pray for them . . . which thou hast given me . . . that they may be one, as we are" (17:9, 11), and other quotations can be understood today in terms of the Revival of Cabala. That is what he is talking about in the Logion: the unity of the "inner" (the contained, the germ) and the "outer" (the container, the shell); the unity of the two aspects (male-female) of Energy, and so on.

When we understand those words, we see how mistaken are those who attempt to "spiritualize" the flesh, or those who (in India, for example) pray that they should be led from the duality into the unity.

All the stages of Consciousness sum up and constitute the Cosmic Consciousness, from their "sleep" in stones to their "awake state" in Reb Yhshwh. And I do not think that any special training is needed to understand the "seeing with one eye" or "with two." I have often mentioned the fact that practically everybody thinks in one direction only. This is easy to see. And there is also this to see: when our soul testifies for us, it gives us a multiple view of things and a permanency of timelessness that recreates our psyches. Then life in us blossoms in creativeness and projects entirely new images "in the place of" obsolete images. A world of perpetual gestation is there "in the place of" repetitive patterns that dry up and decay day after day.

> (L. 77) *Jesus said: I am the Light that is above them all, I am the All, the All came forth from Me and the All attained to Me. Cleave a (piece of) wood, I am there; lift up the stone and you will find Me there.*

I positively know that those words must not be put in parallel with the "expansion of consciousness" that some poets or mystics declare to have experienced: being "one with the All" or being in the All "as a drop of the ocean." I do not say that such experiences are delusions: I don't know. Perhaps they happen. But except for a sense of bliss they are said to give the persons concerned, I have never seen that they result in anything else.

From the point of view of "the two-way traffic" between the universal Energy and the response to it from a living body, the Rabbi goes one way and those mystics go in the opposite direction. I mean that the Rabbi, in his utterances, speaks as the Cosmic Consciousness speaking through him (and, if you remember, astonished at being there), and not as the individual consciousness of those mystics, "expanding" in the direction of the All. In that fundamental difference is the real nature of Reb Yhshwh, the nature that has brought upon him the name Christ—a name that belittles him.

> (L. 66) *Jesus said: Show me the stone which the builders have rejected; it is the corner-stone.*

I said: Rabbi, I know it and I can show it because you taught me the inner meaning of words. That stone is AB-BEN, meaning stone in its most outer sense. Others want that stone to be Simon, who is said to have been thus called and who built his church on it. Still others say that the stone is Father-Son, and they have built their creed on it. But I can show that it is, in truth, the All in us going in the direction of the most precious thing in the whole Universe—the Holy Freedom, the Sacred Principle of Indetermination.

"It is all that is at stake in the Creation; it is ever-freshness of its life. And, Rabbi, you showed me how to know-not-to-know, which is most difficult. Of course, the builders have rejected that Glory: they build and they build and they disappear and their temples crumble and their remains get buried inside the dust. But your cornerstone is indestructible, because it is that upon which nothing can be built."

> (L. 40) *Jesus said: A vine has been planted without the Father and, as it is not established, it will be pulled up by its roots and be destroyed.*

The ancient science of Cabala says that everything is
with Aleph and that Aleph is with everything. A vine
without the Aleph is a fake. It has no more reality than the
fig tree cursed by the Rabbi. Some people are indignant:
"He cursed it for not having fruit at a season when there
are no figs!" Others don't understand. Perhaps they are not
familiar with fig trees. I happen to be.

One bright day I was walking on the dunes that bor-
der the southern Mediterranean Sea. In a place where nothing but sand could be seen at any distance, I was struck by
the penetrating scent of a fig tree. It was hidden by the
undulation of the dunes, about one-half mile away. I finally reached the spot and saw the tree, splendid, proud, and
vibrating with the reflected light upon its many-colored
leaves. It was absolutely alone. There was no other vegeta-
tion to be seen anywhere, not a blade of grass. There was
dry sand everywhere and that tree and the extraordinary
perfume of its leaves filling the atmosphere. And I thought:
how has that richness come out of dry sand? Indeed it is a
miracle. That fig tree is blessed.

> (L. 83) *Jesus said: The images are manifest to man and
> the Light which is within them is hidden in the Image
> of the Light of the Father. He will manifest himself and
> His Image is concealed by His Light.*

Those words are carefully chosen and are certainly very
accurate. They are in accordance with the general teaching
of Reb YHSHWH, which so often mentions the Light. You
remember John's words about light shining in darkness
and not being received by it.

The disciple always keeps in mind the understanding
that the Rabbi is beyond all understanding. The disciple
never declares that he is a man, he is the Lord, he is the Son
of man, he is the Son of the Father, he is mortal, he is
immortal, and so on. The disciple knows that those definitions are nothing but images. The images hide the Light

within them. But (follow this carefully) that light is hidden in the Image of the Light of the Father. And (follow carefully again) His Image is concealed by His Light.

Can you see it? Yes, the disciple has worded it very carefully:

> (L. 50) *Jesus said: If they say to you: "From where have you originated?", say to them: "We have come from the Light, where the Light has originated through itself. It [stood] and it revealed itself in their image." If they say to you: "(Who) are you?", say: "We are His sons and we are the elect of the Living Father." If they ask you: "What is the sign of your Father in you?", say to them: "It is a movement and a rest."*

The Light has originated through itself. There is no deity having monologued, "Let the Light be." I declare that that is the truth.

Light: AUR: Aleph-Waw-Raysh, is the ever-fertile meeting of timelessness and time; of the infinite and the finite. In its total meaning, it is all that is and all that can be. How can so many people repeat without understanding what they say that this Light is created by a demiurge, a God, or whatever name they care to call it—in other words, by some agent that is outside of this Light, that is not Light itself?

And we, who know that, are indeed the elected sons of the living AUR, originator of the All, which is the All in its self-generating movement and rest. We are the sons of it through our understanding.

> (L. 67) *Jesus said: Whoever knows the All but fails (to know) himself lacks everything.*

Another version of that logion is: *Whoever knows the All and is deprived of himself is deprived of the All.* This second version makes more sense and is not open to discussions as to what is the meaning of "knowing" oneself. The words *to know* have been added by translators without reason. *Whoever knows the All but fails himself lacks everything* could have been enough. The meaning would meet the second version's "deprived of himself."

Anyway, we are not scholars and need not quarrel over words. We can even widen the words *to know* and understand that the All obviously includes myself and that "knowing" myself must mean taking possession of myself, integrating myself. When I do, I come in contact with the many emanations of my Soul throughout history and, symbolically, witness the Rabbi's "Fire" born out of the "Waters."

I mean by those symbols the "Waters" of collectivities; those of churches, groups, traditions; those of all the things that are memorized, repeated, and not really thought through; those of obediences; those of accumulated memories; those of the successive layers of mental substances deposited century after century; those in which the divine sparkle of my Soul, one and multiple, has over and over run the risk of drowning. And many people find their bliss in drowning their own self in the Cosmic Ocean, because they have been taught that their very own and unique self is hateful. Reb YHSHWH is in full agreement with the Hebraic original view that the soul comes to fruition when it is fully individuated and aware of its individuation. If his Second Coming has a reason to occur today, it is to recall us to ourselves as being—each and every one of us—unique and yet multiple in the indefinite number of universes.

Read as it should be read, the Bible is a school of "resistance," not of yielding. The many aggressions of YHWH and of Elohim are tests of resistance. The ever-recurring battles of their "chosen people" against their deity and of the obstinate fight of that deity are tests of resistance. Only in such attritions, however tragic, can the souls "take Fire" and be cognizant of their true nature.

The provocative multiform God of the bible, the provocative Reb YHSHWH, are Life itself, powerful, pitiless for the weak, and more cruel still for those who boast of their own strength. Meekness and devotion are of no avail; pride and self-ambition are worse.

So what are we to do? Were it an easy problem, it would have been solved ages ago. Friends, I give you nothing. I said that Aleph is not quantitative.

(L. 113) *His disciples said to Him: when will the Kingdom come? [Jesus said:] It will not come by expectation; they will not say: "See, here," or "See there." But the Kingdom of the Father is spread upon the earth and men do not see it.*

(L. 10) *Jesus said: I have cast fire upon the world, and see, I guard it until it (the world) is afire.*

(L. 82) *Jesus said: Whoever is near to me is near to the fire, and whoever is far from me is far from the Kingdom.*

Let us stop at that. This epistle of mine is finished, for what I had to say I have said.

Bibliography

Blavatsky, Helena P. "The Stanzas of Dzyan," from Blavatsky, *The Secret Doctrine*, Vol. 1. London: Theosophical Publishing House, 1893. Modern editions are available from Theosophical Publishing House in Wheaton, IL.

Castaneda, Carlos. *Tales of Power*. New York: Pocket Books, 1984.

The Gospel According to Thomas. New York: Harper & Row, 1959.

The Lost Books of the Bible and the Forgotten Books of Eden. New York: Meridian, 1963.

Mead, G. R. S. *The Gnostic Crucifixion*. London & Benares: Theosophical Publishing Society, 1907.

_____. *The Hymn to Jesus*. London & Benares: Theosophical Publishing Society, 1907.

_____. *Pistis Sophia*. London: John M. Watkins, 1955.

Suarès, Carlo, trans. Jack Hirschman. *In Tree II*. Santa Barbara, CA: Christopher Books, 1971.

_____. *Cipher of Genesis*. York Beach, ME: Samuel Weiser, 1992.

_____. *Song of Songs*, trans. George Buchanan. Boston: Shambhala, 1972.

_____. *The Passion of Judas*. Boston: Shambhala, 1973.

_____. *The Spectograms of the Hebrew Alphabet*. Written in collaboration with F. A. Wolf for the American edition.

Toben, B. *Space, Time & Beyond*. New York: Bantam, 1983.

Tompkins, Peter, and Christopher Bird. *The Secret Life of Plants*. New York: HarperCollins, 1989.

Biblical Quotations

Acts 9:3, 108
Acts 28:22, 29

Colossians 2:9–10, 26
I Corinthians 2:2, 97
I Corinthians 3:16, 3
I Corinthians 11:8, 113
I Corinthians 13:12, 69, 125
II Corinthians 3:18, 125
II Corinthians 5:17, 6, 7, 144
II Chronicles 36:17–21, 93

Ecclesiastes 1:2, 70
Ecclesiastes 7:20, 75
Ephesians 5:22–23, 114
Exodus 3:9–10, 84
Exodus 3:14, 50
Exodus 4:22, 27, 87
Exodus 6:1, 85
Exodus 6:2–3, 28
Exodus 10:1, 85
Exodus 10:20, 85
Exodus 20:2, 60
Exodus 20:13, 91
Exodus 24:9–11, 83
Exodus 24:10, 92
Exodus 32:27, 92
Exodus 33:5, 92
Exodus 33:20, 92

Genesis 1:1, 113
Genesis 1:11–12, 97
Genesis 1:21, 97

Genesis 1:24, 56, 97
Genesis 1:25, 97
Genesis 1:26–31, 97
Genesis 2:7, 75
Genesis 2:18–24, 143
Genesis 11, 135
Genesis 12, 135
Genesis 25:26, 70
Genesis 32:24–30, 146
Genesis 32:28, 28
Genesis 32:30, 28

Hebrews 9:11–12, 60

Jeremiah 31:9, 27
John 1:5, 57, 65
John 3:3, 86
John 3:7, 86, 96
John 8:58, 62
John 13:8, 63
John 13:18, 70
John 13:24, 64
John 17:5, 125
John 17:6, 126
John 17:12, 132
John 17:20–26, 127, 129
John 18:10, 64
John 20:25, 26, 73
John 18:26–27, 73
John 21:7, 64
John 21:18, 64
John 21:22, 86
Joshua 34:6, 90

Index

A

Aaqav, 70
Aaron, 83
AB-BEN, 209
abel, 35, 70
Abben, 67
Abihu, 84
Abraham, 28, 61, 135, 190, 207
    cycle, of, 136
Acts of John, 170
Adam, 35, 60, 75, 143, 157, 198
AH-HI, 205
Alchemists, 34
Aleph, 37, 38, 44, 45, 47, 49, 50, 51, 52, 53, 54, 55, 65, 67, 70, 96, 129, 131, 132, 135, 155, 156, 157, 158, 163, 197, 200, 206, 210, 213
aleph-bayt, 51
aleph-beith, 207
aleph-hay-yod-hay, 50
Aleph-in-Blood, 198
aleph-lammed-dallet, 155
aleph-tav, 157
aleph-waw-raysh, 211
alpha, 45
alphabet, 38
    Greek, 36, 45
    Hebrew, 39, 53
anti-semitism, 107
apocalypse, 117, 119
Apocrypha, 36, 184

apostles, 166
Aquarius, 53
Aries, 53
astral body, 26
AUR, 211
aut, 52
autiot, 48, 52, 53, 54
Av, 95
    ninth month, 96
ayn, 52

B

bayt, 44, 45, 47, 49, 50, 51, 53, 135
beith, 50
Belial, 119
beliefs, 6
Ben-Adam, 25, 64, 198, 200
Besant, Annie, 169
beta, 45
beth, 37, 38, 50
betray, 132
beyt, 50
Brahma, 135
bind, 104
Bird, Christopher, 19
birth, 139
    completed, 139
Blavatsky, B. P., 169
Bose, Jagadis Chandre, 19
breath, 52, 75
Buddha, 158

C

cabala, 41, 47, 54, 63, 65, 95, 96, 155, 166, 195, 197, 203, 210
cabalists, 34
Caesarea, 59, 60, 62, 63, 64, 70, 71, 80, 83, 103
Caesarea-Philippi, 44, 57, 86, 104
Cain, 35, 70
Capricorn, 53
cardinal point, 123
Castaneda, Carlos, 26
Cathars, 34
cell, 55, 96
Ceretus, 171
Charimus, Leucius, 170
Christ, 6, 7, 158
Christian Era, 71, 183
collective creativity, 141
consciousness, 2, 7, 19, 23, 74, 100, 107, 125, 138, 155, 195, 199
    cosmic, 28, 63, 75, 117, 118, 125, 136, 196, 208, 209
    mystery of, 130
contradiction, 63, 76, 99, 100, 109, 119, 150
corpse, 195
cosmic energy, 21, 28, 38, 39, 41, 91, 107, 129, 132, 168, 183, 185, 200, 201, 203
cosmic vocation, 89
creed, 5

cross, 86, 118
crucifixion, 64, 77, 124
Cyrus, 61

D

dallet, 45, 51, 53
dalleth, 44
damnation, 132
Daniel, 94
Dead Sea Scrolls, 34, 59
death, 6, 8, 75, 138, 161
delta, 45
demon, 119
Descent of Christ in Hell, 195
devil, 104, 119
devotion, 213
djimel, 53
docetism, 165, 167
docetists, 166
Doresse, Jean, 184

E

ego, 66
Ehiay Asher Ehiay, 50
Einstein, Albert, 47
elements, 16
Elias, 63, 76
Elijah, 76
Elohim, 35, 143, 212
emotionalism, 129
energy, 197
enlightenment, rational, 169

Jesus, 1, 7, 10, 21, 25, 37, 42,
44, 59, 61, 69, 90, 99,
131, 132
John, 63, 64, 123
John the Baptist, 90, 99
Jona, 83
Joseph, 37, 90
Joshua, 92
Judah, 44
Judas, 57, 64, 66, 70, 83, 97,
132, 200
Jupiter, 53

K

Kaf, 45, 52, 53
Khaf, 53
King Cyrus of Persia, 94
kingdom, 187
knowing oneself, 188
Krishna, 158

L

lammed, 45, 52, 129, 132, 155
Last Supper, 63
Laws of Moses, 5, 112
Leo, 53
letter-numbers, 44, 45, 51
Libra, 54
life-death, 89, 192
light, 16, 197, 210, 211
love God, 153
Luther, Martin, 31

M

Maccabean revolts, 94
Manichaeus, 165
Manicheists, 166
Marx, Karl, 85, 169
Mars, 53
Massadah, 94
Matter without Spirit, 198
Matthew, 123
Matthias, 57
Mead, G. R. S., 61, 169, 171
meditations, 186
meekness, 213
mem, 45, 47, 52, 135
Mercury, 54
Messiah, 59
metaphysical formula, 89
Moon, 19, 54
Moses, 28, 63, 76, 83, 84, 90,
92
Moshay, 90
mother, 206, 207
Mount Olympus, 66, 81
mustard-seed, 187
Myriam, 204
mysterium ecclesia, 111
mystery, 150
mystics, 96

N

Nadab, 83
new era, 15
Noah, 119
not-dying to oneself, 81

noun, 45, 52, 55, 56, 67
numbers, 38

O

occultists, 34
One Energy, 204
One in Unity, 129
Ophites, 166
Order of Malta, 34
original sin, 1, 75

P

Pan, 59
parables, 191
past, 7
Paul, 5, 21, 22, 26, 29, 66,
    69, 76, 81, 91, 99, 108,
    114, 125, 126, 144, 165,
    170
pay, 52, 54
perfection, 154
Peter, 7, 21, 42, 44, 56, 57,
    61, 63, 64, 66, 67, 71,
    73, 80, 81, 83, 85, 92,
    97, 103, 104, 105, 107,
    109, 111, 114, 126
    as Pharaoh, 97
petrifaction, 8
Pharaoh, 90, 97
phay, 54
Pisces, 53
Pistis Sophia, 61
Plato, 10, 43, 44
Pontius Pilate, 13

poor in spirit, 8, 16
pride, 213
Principle of
    Indetermination, 55,
    142, 202, 209
Priscillianists, 166
propositions, eight, 137
    eighth, 161
    fifth, 153
    fourth, 149
    second, 143
    seventh, 157
    sixth, 155
    third, 145
psyche, 20, 21

Q

qof, 45, 52

R

Rabbi, 5, 27, 28, 29, 33, 36,
    41, 56, 57, 59, 60, 62,
    63, 64, 65, 66, 67, 70,
    71, 74, 76, 79, 83, 84,
    85, 89, 90, 95, 97, 99,
    100, 103, 108, 109, 112,
    115, 126, 129, 130, 136,
    165, 166, 167, 200
Raca, 10
Rachel, 70
raesh, 45
raysh, 45, 52, 54, 135
raysh-sheen, 54
Reb Aqivah, 95

APPENDIX D

Monographs

Now that the story of the seminary has been told in the primary document, there remains much additional material that deserves to supplement what has already appeared. Under seven headings, the major areas of program, structure, and administration are spelled out with specificity and detail beyond what was possible before. The seminary is prepared to share its inner workings, dilemmas, and frustrations with anyone interested. And at the same time, it is eager to enter into dialogue with those engaged in the task of theological education in the context of the urban world.

The monographs are as follows:

I. *Pedagogy: The Scope and Rationale of the Various Programs*
II. *The Constituency of New York Theological Seminary*
III. *Particular Seminary Programs*
IV. *The Administrative Faculty: The Search for Collegiality*
V. *Finances of New York Theological Seminary*
VI. *The Trustee Pattern*
VII. *Cooperative and Dispersed Programs*
VIII. *The History of Biblical Seminary: 1900–1965*

These monographs are readily available from:
New York Theological Seminary
5 West 29th Street
New York, NY 10001

149